MORE Authority in PRAYER.

RESTORING FOUNDATIONS

FOR
INTERCESSOR WARRIORS

JAMES A. DURHAM

TABLE OF CONTENTS

❧❧

PREFACE

❧❧

*I*n Central Texas, where we were residing at that time, a debilitating drought had fallen like a dark pall across the land. The situation had gone past critical months before, and the prospects of relief seemed beyond our reach. People had started to pray with an intensity seldom seen in the past. Even unbelievers were crying out to God for rain. What seemed like a Biblical famine had fallen on a people already suffering loss from the crash of the housing market and an ever growing international financial crisis. The only rain we were seeing was a downpour of heartache and pain from the flood of foreclosures on homes and businesses. People began to speak aloud their previously hidden fears of a season of famine! Desperation seemed to be moving in on people who normally saw the silver lining in every dark cloud. Many people began to look to the intercessors as they had never looked before. Some were even speaking of another kind of famine — a famine of the Word of God which seemed to have fallen on these desperate people. Preachers began to turn again to the ancient prophecies of Amos.

> *"'Behold, the days are coming,' says the Lord God, That I will send a famine on the land, Not a famine of bread, Nor a thirst for water, But of hearing the words of the Lord. They shall wander from sea to sea, and from north*

to east; They shall run to and fro, seeking the word of the Lord, But shall not find it.'" (Amos 8:11-12)

One day, I looked out over a dried up Lake Travis which had once been a beautiful and bountiful body of water. It had not only supplied many communities with life sustaining water, but was also a place for thousands to experience recreation and entertainment. On that day, all I could see was a tiny stream meandering through the exposed bottom of the lake. As I surveyed this pathetic scene, I remembered Israel's Red Sea crossing. The people went across the sea on dry land. As I looked across the lake that morning, it appeared that I could walk across it on dry ground. The children of Israel picked up twelve stones to make a monument to the Lord's provision for them. I thought about going down to the Lake and picking up twelve stones. But I was planning to place them in what remained of the water in order to walk across without getting my feet wet. The situation was desperate! Where were the intercessors? Where were the people willing to build a wall and stand in the gap to save us from the Lord's righteous judgment?

Have you experienced a time like that? Have you been in a situation where you looked for hope, but found none? Have you experienced a time when it seemed that your prayers were not being heard, and then wondered if anyone was even listening to your desperate cries for help? This was the type of season we were in when the Lord began to speak to me about foundation stones for intercessors.

This word from the Lord didn't come in one moment of blinding insight. It emerged slowly as a progressive revelation over a period of more than three years. It was early Spring, 2009, when the Lord began to speak to me about these foundation stones for intercessors. During this season, I visited with a number of people who identified themselves as intercessors. They told me stories about going through many serious problems which they identified as enemy attacks. The challenges they were facing were serious indeed. Some had experienced life threatening accidents, illnesses and injuries. Others had entered into a period of deep emotional pain requiring them to be hospitalized. The more I listened the more clearly I could see that somehow a spirit of fear had moved in and captured many of the Lord's intercessors. This just didn't seem right to me. What could be happening to cause dedicated and experienced intercessors to lapse into a fear based religious system? I don't believe that our loving and faithful Father God does things like that to His beloved children. As I meditated on this, I remembered Paul's words to His spiritual son Timothy.

> *"Therefore I remind you to stir up the gift of God which is in you through the laying on of my hands. For God has not given us a spirit of fear, but of power and of love and of a sound mind."* (2 Timothy 1:6-7)

Something seemed very wrong about God's people being so vulnerable to the attacks of a defeated and vanquished enemy. It seemed to me that we needed to stir up our spiritual gifts, cast off the spirit of fear, and embrace the power, love, and soundness of mind Paul spoke about to Timothy. I wanted to see a change. I wanted to hear people giving testimonies to the power and miraculous working of Jesus Christ, my victorious savior, rather than confessing the power of the enemy. I began to pray to the Lord for wisdom and understanding. The Lord's answer came in the form of a call for me to focus on the foundation stones He had established for those He had called and anointed as intercessor warriors.

My first revelation from the Lord came with the identification of five of these foundation stones. I developed this revelation from the Lord into a sermon series simply titled, "***Intercessor – Warriors***!" A small challenge arose in my mind. I wanted to approach this using my reason and logic. This was a mistake. I couldn't understand how I could make a rectangular foundation with an odd number of stones. I wanted to be able to draw a picture of this foundation as a way of assisting others to better understand what I was trying to teach. The Lord didn't dignify my question with an answer. I believe there are two reasons why He didn't answer at that time. First, I was still thinking in the natural instead of seeing it from a spiritual position. Additionally, this revelation was not yet complete in His timing.

As I continued to develop this sermon series, I became aware in my spirit that there should be seven foundation stones. I waited for the revelation of the other two stones. In the meantime, I continued with the sermon series. I went through this series with two churches all the while believing there was more to come. It was a little over a year later that the Lord revealed two more stones to me. I was pleased to receive what I thought was the fullness of this revelation. However, this still left me with the original dilemma. How do you make a rectangular foundation with an odd number of stones? I was happy to get the identification of these additional stones even though I didn't get any word about my personal challenge.

I have always liked the number seven because of the prophetic significance of that number. In the Bible the number seven means completeness or fullness. Having seven stones in the foundation for intercessors seemed to speak of the completeness of this revelation. It seemed to say, "This is all you need!" I like things that are complete. I like things that provide all I need. I was content at that time and convinced that this was all I was looking for.

Then the Lord spoke to me telling me to develop this into a training package and write a book about these foundation stones. Over a period of several months, I completed the first part of this project by developing the training. Shortly after this, I received an invitation to teach it in January in the city of Chicago. This was like getting good news and bad news at the same time. The good news was that I was excited about the opportunity to teach, because I knew this would help me in writing the book. In addition, it was good because I wanted to be obedient to the Lord's command. The bad news was that I would be going to Chicago in January. After sixteen years in Texas and two years in South Carolina, I was not prepared for winter in the north-central part of the United States. However, I agreed to meet the request. Shortly after I agreed to teach and by the grace of God, this training conference was delayed until April.

As I had hoped and prayed, conducting the training in Chicago was a great learning experience for me in preparation for writing this book. However, it was another good news/bad news experience. I received many revelations from the Lord as I prepared to speak and I received more as His anointing fell on me during each session. That was very good news. It was an answer to my hopes and prayers, but then the bad news came. As I sat down just before the last session, the Lord gave me two more foundation stones. I responded to this gift (it truly was a gift) with an exasperated response. I said, *"But, Lord what about the number seven? I've already named the training and the book, "Seven Foundation Stones for Intercessor Warriors!"* The Lord said, *"Get over it!"* I responded by saying, *"Yes Sir! I will do it because you say so!"*

I had the opportunity in this situation to see the powerful way the Lord can work without having to explain Himself. I was inspired by the Spirit to go to my notes on Biblical numbers and look up the prophetic meaning of the number nine. When I searched through my notes, I made a wonderful discovery. The number nine has a similar meaning to the number seven. It also means completeness of fullness, but with an added idea. It is divine completeness. The number seven means spiritual fullness. The number nine means divine perfection. If the Lord is building the foundation, you know it is going to be perfect and will reflect the fullness of His work. I started to get excited about this number nine and the revelation the Lord had released to me. I noticed that nine is three times three. It is like a multiplication of who God is and what He can do. Hallelujah! My concern was lifted like a vapor.

However, I still had that other problem. How can you build a rectangular foundation with an odd number of stones? Then the Lord said, *"Don't you know that I have already revealed that to you! Remember what I showed you during your visit to Israel in 2010?"* I am realizing more and more that the reason the Lord doesn't answer my questions is because He has already given the answer and for some reason I wasn't paying attention. I began to think about that visit to Israel and tried to remember how He had answered my prayer. Then it came to me! We had visited the Temple Mount on that tour, and we had gone to the Western Wall several different times to pray. On one of those visits, we had been invited by our friend Carol Basile to go on a tour of the excavation under the Western Wall. During this tour many of my questions had been answered, but, at that time, I had only understood and acknowledged the answers to things in the natural.

On an earlier visit to the Temple Mount, our tour guide had explained that the foundation of the Temple was not built on the ground. As I looked at the massive stone foundation, I wondered how that could be possible. The weight of the stones is beyond my understanding. How could they build something so massive and so heavy without it being on the ground? The guide explained that in the Jewish culture there is a belief that bones defile the ground. Consequently the foundation of the Temple could not be resting on potentially defiled soil. Mount Moriah had been there since the creation and many primitive groups had lived there, fought there, and could have buried people there. In order to insure that the Temple foundation would not be defiled, they had built a very large complex of stone arches to hold up the foundation. Each of these arches was built up from bedrock with no dirt in between. Now, only these arches and the air between them are under the foundation of the Temple.

As we went on the tour underground next to the western wall, we were able to see many of those massive stone arches. In fact, we walked under several of them. They were so amazing. I remember one which must have been 40-50 feet high. What really amazed me was that these arches are as strong and solid today as they were when first built thousands of years ago. This seemed to be a powerful revelation of what the Lord can do in our lives. When people are willing to follow the inspiration and directions of the Lord, something strong and permanent is built. I don't know of any other structure in the world which has gone through all the tribulation of war and natural disasters like the Temple Mount and still remained completely solid and secure. It is as rock solid today as it was in the days of Solomon. Wow! God is amazing! But, I still didn't understand what this had to do with my question? In what way had the Lord answered me about the foundation stones for intercessors?

Suddenly, the revelation came. The Lord is calling us to build a solid foundation of faith for the kingdom of God. This foundation is held up by many arches representing different aspects of His work. One of these arches is made up of the foundation stones for intercession. Arches are always built with an odd number of stones. The final stone in an arch is called the "capstone." This stone is shaped like a wedge and the pressure from this stone holds all the other stones in place. The weight of this stone presses down on all the stones below giving them greater overall strength.

As I searched through the Bible to learn more about the Lord's foundations, I saw another powerful prophetic word revealed in the NIV version. I made this surprising discovery as I studied references to the "*stone rejected by the builders.*" Seven times the NIV translation identifies this stones as the "*the capstone.*" Up to this point, I had been trying to visualize and understand Jesus as the cornerstone of a two dimensional and rectangular shaped foundation, but the Lord wanted me to understand his revelation as the stones in an arch supporting the foundation. The foundation for intercessor warriors is like one of those powerful support systems under the Temple Mount.

If you would like to study this for yourself, here is a quick list of the seven references from the English version of the NIV Bible: Psalm 118:22, Zechariah 4:7, Matthew 21:42, Mark 12:10, Luke 20:17, Acts 4:11, and 1 Peter 2:7. As I went over these passages several times, I suddenly became aware of the significance of what the Lord had prepared for us. You may have already seen it. Did you take note of the fact that there are seven references in the Bible to the *"capstone?"* Remember that seven is the number of spiritual completion or fullness. This is no accident. The Lord knows exactly what this means for you and me. Peter saw it and summed up the Lord's revelation this way:

> *"Now to you who believe, this stone is precious. But to those who do not believe, 'The stone the builders rejected has become <u>the capstone</u>,'"* (1 Peter 2:7, NIV)

Is Jesus your *"capstone?"* Is He the strong foundation of the Lord upon which your hope and faith is built? My goal for you in reading this book is that you will find and begin to stand on all these stones so that you can be firmly planted as an Intercessor Warrior in the kingdom of God. As you stand on His sure foundation, I decree that you will no longer be subject to the kinds of enemy attacks which you may have experienced in the past. I decree that through the authority and power given to you by Jesus Christ, you will fully experience victory over all the power of the enemy. I decree that you will experience being more than a conqueror through Him who loves you.

> *"Yet in all these things we are more than conquerors through Him who loved us. For I am persuaded that*

neither death nor life, nor angels nor principalities nor powers, nor things present nor things to come, nor height nor depth, nor any other created thing, shall be able to separate us from the love of God which is in Christ Jesus our Lord." (Romans 8:37-39)

ACKNOWLEDGEMENTS

✂✂

*T*here is never any real accomplishment purely through the work of one person. It is the Lord who gives us the ability and the inspiration to do His work. This is especially true in the area of writing books about what the Lord is calling us to do for the kingdom of God. I want to give first priority to thanking the Lord for the inspiration, revelation, and help I received in completing this work. To be honest, He deserves something over ninety-nine percent of the credit.

I also want to acknowledge the amazing help I received from my extremely blessed, highly favored, and anointed wife, Gloria. Without her inspiration, encouragement, and assistance this book could never have been completed. I want to also acknowledge my daughter, Michelle, who was a constant and consistent cheerleader throughout the process. When faced with challenges and difficulties, I had only to turn to either of these two wonderful ladies for inspiration and encouragement. I am so thankful to the Lord that He has placed them in my life and constantly blesses me through their love and support!

I am grateful to Pastor Huh, Chul, of Pal Bok Presbyterian Church in Chicago, for providing an opportunity for me to teach these lessons to the valiant intercessor warriors who bravely go into battle daily to stand against the enemy and build up the kingdom of God. I am grateful to many others who have encouraged and supported me in the many months required to complete this project. I cannot mention all, but give a special word of thanks to our spiritual daughters and ministry partners Mia Nolen, and MiSo Yun. I am also grateful to the members of King of Kings Church in DaeJeon, Korea, and especially to Pastor (Dr.) Tae-gil Ahn for giving me the opportunity to conduct this training in Korea. You have each been a blessing and inspiration, and I will always be grateful.

INTRODUCTION

𝔞 re you an intercessor? Are you an intercessor warrior?
I believe that all the faithful and powerful intercessors
are truly warriors who draw the battle lines against an ancient
enemy in the greatest battle ever fought on and for planet earth.
If you are an intercessor warrior you are part of an elite force
called by the Lord to take your stand with Him to save mankind. Remember the Lord is also an intercessor warrior. He is
a mighty intercessor for you and for me. *"It is Christ who died,
and furthermore is also risen, who is even at the right hand
of God, who also makes intercession for us."* (Romans 8:34).
The Holy Spirit is another intercessor warrior of the highest
magnitude.

> *"Likewise the Spirit also helps in our weaknesses. For
> we do not know what we should pray for as we ought, but
> the Spirit Himself makes intercession or us with groan-
> ings which cannot be uttered. Now He who searches the
> hearts knows what the mind of the Spirit is, because He
> makes intercession for the saints according to the will of
> God."* (Romans 8:26-27)

In addition to the Lord Jesus and the Holy Spirit, the Bible
gives us the names of many powerful intercessors in both the
Old and New Testaments. One of my favorites is Epaphras, a

companion and fellow warrior with the Apostle Paul. We don't know that much about Epaphras. He was only mentioned a few times in the Bible. But I like what I understand about him. He was a prayer warrior! I recommend that you study the two passages below and draw out as much revelation knowledge as possible from the life and ministry of Epaphras.

> "__*Epaphras*__*, who is one of you, a bondservant of Christ, greets you, always laboring fervently for you in prayers, that you may stand perfect and complete in all the will of God. For I bear him witness that he has a great zeal for you, and those who are in Laodicea, and those in Hierapolis.*" (Colossians 4:12-13)

> "*We give thanks to the God and Father of our Lord Jesus Christ, praying always for you, since we heard of your faith in Christ Jesus and of your love for all the saints; because of the hope which is laid up for you in heaven, of which you heard before in the word of the truth of the gospel, which has come to you, as it has also in all the world, and is bringing forth fruit, as it is also among you since the day you heard and knew the grace of God in truth; as you also learned from* __*Epaphras*__*, our dear fellow servant, who is a faithful minister of Christ on your behalf, who also declared to us your love in the Spirit.*" (Colossians 1:3-8)

At the beginning of this year, I began to hear the lord saying: "*It is time to restore the foundations!*" When He first spoke this to me, it sounded great. I liked it, but I didn't fully understand what the Lord meant. In response to this word, I asked, "*Lord, What does that mean?*" For a long time, I didn't receive an answer. So, I waited on Him. Then He spoke the same words again, "*It is time to restore the foundations!*" Once more, I asked Him to help me understand fully what He meant by this directive? His only reply was to say again, *"It is time to restore the foundations!"*

Something I have learned over the years is that when the Lord tells me something over and over, I need to listen! When the Lord tells us something two or three times, it normally means that it is fixed and certain. When the Lord does this, He is issuing a directive! He is clearly saying that in this season we need to be involved in restoring foundations. I understood this, but I still needed more information. There are so many different types of foundations. There are foundations for physical buildings. There are foundational concepts for every workable theory. There are foundational principles behind businesses, churches, and social organizations. The list could go on and on. I wanted to know more specifically what the Lord was talking about before launching a study, a sermon series, or a book. So, I kept asking for more information from the Lord, but none seemed to be given. He kept giving me the same directive.

What do you do when the Lord tells you something over and over, but you don't understand it fully? I don't know what you do, but when I get a command without explanation, I turn to the Word of God. I went to my electronic Bible and did a search on the word "foundation." In the New King James Version of the Bible, I found 55 references to this word. As I looked at that result, I started to get more and more excited about what the Lord was saying. The number five always points me to the five-fold offices of ministry which the Lord established for His church. I started to reflect on the foundations for these five offices of ministry.

After spending some time reflecting on these things, I looked at the prophetic meaning of the number five. It is consistently viewed as the number for God's grace (atonement, eternal life, the cross). I began to reflect on the foundations of God's grace and goodness. The foundations of God's work are all solid and permanent. The finished work of Christ is the foundation for God's grace toward us. This foundation does not need to be restored, but perhaps our teaching on these topics does need to go through some restoration.

I also noted that the number of references (55) represented a double portion of these blessings from the Lord. I like the idea of double portions. I want a double portion of His out-pouring of health, provision, grace, and spiritual gifts. This idea of double portions began to speak to me of how solid the Lord wanted the foundations to be. It should be established in a way that will support the weight of all He wants to do in our lives, families, and ministries.

I decided to extend my word search on the computer Bible and looked for references to the word "foundations." I found 33 references in the New King James Version of the Bible. This was really getting interesting. There was another double number which could represent another double portion out-pouring from the Lord. I reflected on the prophetic meaning of the number three. There are three persons in the trinity: Father, Son, and Holy Spirit. It is the number of divine perfection and divine completeness. There is nothing about this foundation which needs to be restored.

Another revelation came. We are created in God's image and so many things in our natural realm are in groups of three. God created three types of matter (animal, vegetable, and mineral). There are three parts to our personal makeup (spirit, soul, and body). God divided time for us into three parts (past, present, and future). Grammatically there are three persons in our speech (me, myself, and I). There are three types of human ability (word, thought, and deed). Even though these are in the natural realm, there is very little that we can restore in these areas.

As I prepared to do a lesson on restoring foundations, I wrote: "When the Lord brings something up 88 times, I listen." At this point I paused to look at that number. It was another double number which seemed very significant. I really like the number eight which is almost universally viewed as the number of new beginnings. Our God is the God of new beginnings and it is awesome to see all the variety of newness in His work.

> *"Then He who sat on the throne said, 'Behold, I make all things new.' And He said to me, "Write, for these words are true and faithful."* (Revelation 21:5)

It is important to remember, that numbers are significant to the Lord. Hold that thought for a moment and add to it another important concept: There are no accidents in the Bible. When it comes to God's Word, we may not always understand everything, but as time goes by, we see more and more of His intentionality in every word of Scripture. There is nothing in the Bible that will cause the Lord to say, "Oops! I didn't see that coming!" or to say, "That surprises me! I didn't know that!" Sometimes, I'm surprised, but God is never surprised. He does everything with purpose and perfection.

It has been my goal for a long time to study through the Bible several times each year. I don't just read or scan through it quickly. I'm talking about studying all of the content of different versions with a wide variety of footnotes. I have a holy hunger for His Word, and it is like rich food for my soul. As I read it over and over, I underline it, highlight it, and write notes in the margins. Even after 30-40 times through it, I find myself saying, *Wow! Did you see that!*

The more time you spend in God's Word, the more He will open it up to you. Inspiration comes from the Lord and He responds to perspiration on our part. The more we put into it, the more He releases supernaturally to us. There are things you can't really see today, but tomorrow He will give you in-depth revelation knowledge about these same things. I recommend that you stay in the Word! Never allow yourself to think that you have enough of it or that you know it all. No matter how long you have been at the study, God can give so much more!

The number eight is the number seven (fullness or completeness) plus one. After things are complete, the next step is something new. Our God is one who is constantly doing new things; making new things; and establishing new beginnings. I love Father God, and I am so happy that He is who He is! I have needed many new beginnings in my lifetime, and He has always been there to make it happen. I am so very grateful to this awesome and wonderful God of ours!

When the Lord gives you a revelation or prophetic word accompanied by the number eight, it indicates that you have already received the fullness of one area of His plan, and now you are moving into something new. Seeing the two eights together refers to a double portion of new beginnings. Over and over this year the Lord has spoken to me about releasing things in double portions. Why not in the area of new beginnings? It makes perfect sense when you look deeply into God's attributes. He is the one who blesses in such abundance that it spills over into the lives of others. Remember the blessing of Abraham. God called him to step out of his comfort zone and step into a new beginning. The Lord promised that in every aspect of his life Abram would be blessed so richly that all the families on earth would be blessed.

> *"Now the Lord had said to Abram: 'Get out of your country, from your family And from your father's house, To a land that I will show you. I will make you a great nation; I will bless you And make your name great; And you shall be a blessing. I will bless those who bless you, And I will curse him who curses you; And in you all the families of the earth shall be blessed.'"* (Genesis 12:1-3)

The family of man was still young on the earth and the Lord had already called on Abraham to move into a new beginning. Not long after this new beginning, the blessing of the Lord had already made him very wealthy. (*"Abram was very rich in livestock, in silver, and in gold."* (Genesis 13:2)] As Abram faithfully obeyed God, the extent of the blessings in this "new beginning" started to be revealed.

> *"No longer shall your name be called Abram, but your name shall be Abraham; for I have made you a father of many nations. I will make you exceedingly fruitful; and I will make nations of you, and kings shall come from you. And I will establish My covenant between Me and you and your descendants after you in their generations, for an everlasting covenant, to be God to you and your descendants after you. Also I give to you and your descendants after you the land in which you are a stranger, all the land of Canaan, as an everlasting possession; and I will be their God."* (Genesis 17:5-8)

For Abraham this was a progressive revelation. God gave him the first part of the vision, and as he was faithful and obedient, more was given. Gradually the extent of God's plan for Abraham was revealed. It would have been too much for him to grasp in the beginning. God worked with Abraham step by step to get him to the fullness of the blessing.

I believe that the Lord is positioning people right now in order to offer them a profound new beginning. These new beginnings will be so awesome that they will need to be released progressively and in double portions. Like Abraham, people will have a difficult time grasping all that the Lord has planned for them in just one revelation or in one portion. As with Abraham, God requires people to operate in faith, patience, and obedience as these things manifests. You will have to believe it in order to receive it.

> *"By faith Abraham obeyed when he was called to go out to the place which he would receive as an inheritance. And he went out, not knowing where he was*

going. By faith he dwelt in the land of promise as in a foreign country, dwelling in tents with Isaac and Jacob, the heirs with him of the same promise; for he waited for the city which has foundations, whose builder and maker is God." (Hebrews 11:8-10)

The kind of faith the writer of the book of Hebrews is talking about is not merely a passive belief system. It is much more than a casual comment about believing that God exists or Jesus is Lord. The writer is talking about the kind of life changing faith that grabs hold of your spirit with such awesome force that you will never be the same again. You have to step out on a revelation like that to step into your destiny. Abraham had to step out on faith, leave his family, friends, and familiar surroundings, and move into something new with nothing but the promises of God.

Abraham took that leap of faith into his new beginning. How about you? Are you ready to step out on faith and move into a new beginning with nothing but the promises of God? Are you ready to take action on His promises? When you get a prophetic word, you have to reach out and take it for it to be effective. You don't just hold on to prophesies and expect them to manifest without your action. When you get a prophetic word, you need to step into it! You need to move forward with it.

Sometimes, you may not be able to see where you are going, but you step out in faith. You simply trust that when you step out in faith, God will be there for you. You believe beyond doubt that He will lead you to the next step. He will lead you step by step into the fullness of His blessing for you.

Are there some areas in your life where you would like to experience a new beginning? I believe that most people would like to have one or more new beginnings? Most people in these times of economic challenges would like some new beginnings for things they may have lost. As I have shared this word in various conferences this year, I discovered that most people are hoping and praying for new beginnings. Here are a few which are representative of these requests:

1. New beginnings for businesses
2. New beginnings for finances
3. New beginnings for homes after foreclosures
4. New money for depleted IRAs and lost investments
5. New beginnings from miraculous healings and the release of divine health
6. New beginnings for broken relationships
7. New beginnings in relationships with the Lord

Something else pretty amazing began to happen just after the first of the year. It seemed like everywhere I travelled people were asking me the same question. Many of these people didn't really know very much about me. But, they were all asking the same question: *"What are you hearing from the Lord lately?"* I always answered; *The Lord is telling me to restore foundations!* Then something else amazing happened. These people were reporting that the Lord was also telling them about foundations. Over and over, I got the same amazing response.

As we shared what we were hearing, we began to realize that our amazing Father God was saying something different to each of us. The topic is too big for one person or one prophetic word. What God plans to do will require that many of us respond to Him in faith and then do our individual part of the overall plan. We are unique and God deals with us that way. The common denominator for all of us is the Lord's focus on foundations.

This is a good reminder that when we share with others and exchange the revelations we are receiving from the Lord, we get a wider perspective on the Lord's Word. In sharing what the Lord is doing in each of our lives, we build one another up in our faith and understanding. That is what happened for those of us who shared what the Lord was saying about foundations. Our sharing expanded the meaning for each of us. This experience convinced me that we need to be more consistent in sharing. Perhaps the Lord has been speaking to you about foundations. Find someone and share your revelations with them. Let the Lord surprise you and build you up by what He is revealing to others.

Once again I heard God say, "*It is time to restore the foundations!*" I went to the Word and studied each of the references to foundations. I quickly learned how specific and detailed the Lord is about foundations.

FOUNDATIONS ARE IMPORTANT TO THE LORD

The Bible tells us that, the Lord established everything in his creation on solid foundations. He set up foundations for the overall creation and for each part of it as well. Did you know that there are even foundations for the heavens?

"The earth trembled and quaked, the foundations of the heavens shook; they trembled because he was angry."
(2 Samuel 22:8)

In spite of my investment of time, study, and prayer, I could not get a mental picture of the foundations of the heavens. As I continued to reflect on this, it became clear that this was not the area I was to focus on. The Lord alone is able to keep and maintain the foundations of heaven. So, I turned my attention to the earth as I remembered and reflected on the teaching from the Lord in Psalm 115:16, "*The heaven, even the heavens, are the Lord's; But the earth He has given to the children of men.*" Pause and think about this as we dig deeper into this revelation. Did you know that there are foundations for the earth?

"The valleys of the sea were exposed and the founda-
tions of the earth laid bare at the rebuke of the Lord, at
the blast of breath from his nostrils." (2 Samuel 22:16)

Again, I applied myself in order to understand if this was
what the Lord was saying to me. I had the same experience as
I had in trying to understand the foundations of the heavens.
In the natural, there is simply no way to understand this. We
know from our studies of science that there are some known
and some hidden forces which hold our little planet in its orbit
around the Sun. We know that the Lord has done something
very amazing by setting it up and keeping it in the exact same
orbit so that we will not be drawn into the Sun and burn up
or get so far from the Sun that it will be too cold to maintain
human life. These things are amazing in themselves, but none
of the passages of scripture clearly identify or define actual
foundations for the earth.

Further study brought light on additional kinds of foundations. The new heaven and new earth will be built on an
amazing foundation. I went to the Word to look more closely
at the awesome promises of the Lord for these divine foundations.

"Now the wall of the city had twelve foundations, and
on them were the names of the twelve apostles of the
Lamb." (Revelation 21:14)

As I considered this idea, I got excited about the connection with the twelve apostles. The twelve apostles stood on the
foundation of faith and their names will be memorialized in the
foundation of the New Jerusalem. God is so good. He never
forgets what you have done or what you have to give up in
order to, serve Him by proclaiming the gospel of the kingdom.
The work of the apostles will be remembered throughout all
eternity. Look closely at the description of these foundations.

"The foundations of the wall of the city were adorned with all kinds of precious stones: the first foundation was jasper, the second sapphire, the third chalcedony, the fourth emerald, the fifth sardonyx, the sixth sardius, the seventh chrysolite, the eighth beryl, the ninth topaz, the tenth chrysoprase, the eleventh jacinth, and the twelfth amethyst." (Revelation 21:19-20)

The foundations are made of precious stones. We are being told that there will be nothing ordinary about the New Jerusalem to include the stones of the foundations. I believe that in this account, the Lord is giving us a picture of the importance of all the foundations in His Word. We may not understand the nature of these foundations. But we know they are very important to the Lord.

I also believe that all of these references to foundations and precious stones are prophetic words for us. They lead us to understand that everything the Lord does is built on a strong foundation. Even the throne on which He sits has foundations. As I studied further, I noticed how consistent the Lord has been in describing His foundations. Consider the two biblical references below concerning the foundations of His throne.

"Righteousness and justice are the foundation of Your throne; Mercy and truth go before Your face." (Psalm 89:14)

"Clouds and darkness surround Him; Righteousness and justice are the foundation of His throne." (Psalm 97:2)

These verses were written by two different authors over a long period of time. Yet, the message is totally consistent. Righteousness and justice are the foundation of His throne. From our perspective (in the natural) these two things do not seem like stones in a foundation. However, in the spiritual realm, the attributes of God are real substance. It helped me to understand this as I considered Hebrews 11:1, *"Now faith is the substance of things hoped for, the evidence of things not seen."* If faith can be substance and evidence for us, then righteousness and justice can be foundations for a spiritual throne. Perhaps the real problem is that we don't fully understand how faith can be substance. We can only understand it through faith and by the revelation the Holy Spirit gives. It is the same with the attributes of God (righteousness and justice) being foundation stones for His throne.

As you consider your foundations as well as His, remember that He founded our faith on a very strong foundation.

> *"Therefore thus says the Lord God: 'Behold, I lay in Zion a stone for a foundation, a tried stone, a precious cornerstone, a sure foundation; Whoever believes will not act hastily. Also I will make* **justice** *the measuring line, And* **righteousness** *the plummet; The hail will sweep away the refuge of lies, And the waters will overflow the hiding place.'"* (Isaiah 28:16-17)

Now we see something even more interesting and amazing. Not only are justice and righteousness the foundation of God's throne, they are also the foundation for our faith. We need to sharpen our focus and recognize more and more what the Lord is trying to say to us in this season. Are these two attributes of God your foundation? God has given you a very precious foundation stone. He has given you Jesus Christ and He has based your whole experience on who Jesus is and what He has done for you. Can you hear what the Lord is saying? The Lord is saying again: *"It is time to restore the foundations!"* Amen? This message is so timely! The entire world is in desperate need to get back on the foundations of justice and righteousness. Imagine how much the world would change for the better, if we were all back on this solid foundation given by our creator?

The more I studied, the more I found myself being drawn to focus on the Bible's descriptions of the foundation of the Temple. As I studied further, the Lord gave me an additional revelation from the Jewish Bible which I had not seen in the other English translations. This passage made clear that good progress in building foundations and temples (*you are the temple*) comes from listening to the prophetic words released by the Lord through His prophets.

> *"The leaders of the Judeans made good progress with the rebuilding, thanks to the prophesying of Hagai (Haggai) the prophet and Z'kharyah (Zechariah) the son of 'Iddo. They kept building until they were finished, in keeping with the command of the God of Israel and in accordance with the order of Koresh (Cyrus), Daryavesh (Darius) and Artach'shashta (Artaxerxes) king of Persia."* (Ezra 6:14, CJB)

As you are building up and restoring the foundations, remain very aware of the importance of the prophetic words given by the Lord through His prophets. All your work will progress more quickly to completion as you follow the commands of God released through prophesy. Amen!

THE TEMPLE WAS BUILT ON A VERY STRONG FOUNDATION

> *"And the king commanded them to quarry large stones, costly stones, and hewn stones, to lay the foundation of the temple."* (1 Kings 5:17)

I meditated on this verse for several weeks. Have you seen those large stones under the temple mount? Gloria and I were blessed to have the opportunity to go on that tour of the excavation work under the Temple Mount in 2010. As mentioned in the Preface, our very good friend, Carol Basile, made a connection for that tour and invited us to participate. I will always be grateful for that invitation, because it opened up a whole new understanding for me about the type of foundations the Lord calls us to build.

At one point in the tour, we were sitting on stone benches in a large cavern. From this vantage point, we could see the lowest part of the Temple foundation. We were shown one of two gigantic stones in the foundation. I didn't expect to get wowed here, but after seeing them, all I could think to say was, Wow! According to the tour guide, one of those two stone weighs 570 tons (1,140,000 pounds). This one stone weighs more than a fully loaded 747 jetliner. It is a challenge to grasp the magnitude of this stone with our natural minds. This one stone is 13.5 meters long, four meters high and three and half meters thick. The stone next to it was about two thirds of the size of this one. Their combined weight was almost equal to two fully loaded 747 airplanes. These two stones are so huge that an entire Roman legion couldn't move them when the Temple was destroyed in the siege of 70 A.D. For the first time, I understood what I had been reading in two chapters of the second book of Chronicles. Remember that the two sections of scripture below were originally a continuous writing.

> *"Then Solomon numbered all the aliens who were in the land of Israel, after the census in which David his father had numbered them; and there were found to be one hundred and fifty-three thousand six hundred. And he made seventy thousand of them bearers of burdens, eighty thousand stonecutters in the mountain, and three thousand six hundred overseers to make the people work."* (2 Chronicles 2:17-18)

"Now Solomon began to build the house of the Lord at Jerusalem on Mount Moriah, where the Lord had appeared to his father David, at the place that David had prepared on the threshing floor of Ornan [Araunah in 2 Samuel 24:16ff] the Jebusite. And he began to build on the second day of the second month in the fourth year of his reign. This is the foundation which Solomon laid for building the house of God: The length was sixty cubits [by cubits according to the former measure] and the width twenty cubits." (2 Chronicles 3:1-3)

Understanding the magnitude of this project, Solomon selected 70,000 people to carry the stones and 80,000 stone cutters. Consider also what we learn in 1 Kings 6-7, *"And the temple, when it was being built, was built with stone finished at the quarry, so that no hammer or chisel or any iron tool was heard in the temple while it was being built."* Remember those two huge stones which could not be moved by the Roman legion! Solomon's workers carved them in the quarry and carried them up the hill to the Temple Mount. How were they able to do that? We don't have the technology or equipment today to move things that large. Here is another challenging thought. How were they able to position them correctly at the bottom of the foundation with the technology and tools available to them at that time in history? The only answer I can propose is that it was with God's help. The wisdom the Lord gave to Solomon was obviously his primary source for this project.

By themselves these two large stones, which required most of the 70,000 people for carriers, are amazing and awe inspiring. But there is more. There were not only large stones but precious stones and hewn stones in the foundation. A great description is given in the first book of Kings.

"All these were of costly stones cut to size, trimmed with saws, inside and out, from the foundation to the eaves,

*and also on the outside to the great court. The founda-
tion was of costly stones, large stones, some ten cubits
and some eight cubits. And above were costly stones,
hewn to size, and cedar wood. The great court was
enclosed with three rows of hewn stones and a row of
cedar beams. So were the inner court of the house of the
Lord and the vestibule of the temple.*" (1 Kings 7:9-12)

All of this awe inspiring foundation is pointing us to a deep
spiritual reality. We have been given one of those precious
stones. In fact, we have been given the most precious stone
of all. Jesus is our precious cornerstone. Jesus along with the
precious stones of the prophets and apostles have made up a
foundation for us which will endure forever.

*"Therefore it is also contained in the Scripture, 'Behold,
I lay in Zion A chief cornerstone, elect, precious, And
he who believes on Him will by no means be put to
shame.' Therefore, to you who believe, He is precious;
but to those who are disobedient, 'The stone which the
builders rejected Has become the chief cornerstone,'
and 'A stone of stumbling And a rock of offense.' They
stumble, being disobedient to the word, to which they
also were appointed.*" (1 Peter 2:6-8)

You need to make this prophetic word your own. Jesus is
your sure foundation which lasts forever. Isaiah 28:16, *"Therefore thus says the Lord God: 'Behold, I lay in Zion a stone
for a foundation, A tried stone, a precious cornerstone, a sure
foundation; Whoever believes will not act hastily.'"* Read this
aloud a few times and speak it in the first person. Speak and
decree what the Lord is saying: "Jesus is my sure foundation
which will last forever and ever! Amen!"

Solomon was wise enough to build the foundation for his
own house the same way he built it for the Temple. In fact, he

built several houses using this same method and these same kinds of stones. In addition to his personal home, he did it for the House of the Forest of Lebanon and the house for Pharaoh's daughter.

> *"And the house where he dwelt had another court inside the hall, of like workmanship. Solomon also made a house like this hall for Pharaoh's daughter, whom he had taken as wife. All these were of costly stones cut to size, trimmed with saws, inside and out, from the foundation to the eaves, and also on the outside to the great court. The foundation was of costly stones, large stones, some ten cubits and some eight cubits."* (1 Kings 7:8-10)

Considering that he was wise enough to build his house on the same foundation, what should you and I do with this knowledge? I want my house to be on a sure foundation. I want my house to have the precious cornerstone which is Jesus Christ. However, there is something more important here than just our personal hopes and desires. There is a greater purpose behind all this. Get this! We are the temple of God. As the temple of God we need the appropriate foundation with the proper building materials. The really big question right now is: How well is your foundation built?

In buildings today, the foundation often seems like a rush job. I have watched many houses being built. It seems as if we watch on one day as they are pouring the foundation, and the next day the frame of the house has already gone up. I was in a new housing development once where the foundations were crumbling in one area. The homeowners gathered to file suit against the builder. The builder quickly contracted with a company specializing in foundation repair to solve the problem hoping to stop the legal entanglements. It seemed to work, but I didn't think I would feel secure with a 2-3 story house standing on a repaired foundation. It reminded me of the importance of being on solid rock. Then I remember something Jesus taught.

"But why do you call Me 'Lord, Lord,' and not do the things which I say? Whoever comes to Me, and hears My sayings and does them, I will show you whom he is like: He is like a man building a house, who dug deep and laid the foundation on the rock. And when the flood arose, the stream beat vehemently against that house, and could not shake it, for it was founded on the rock. But he who heard and did nothing is like a man who built a house on the earth without a foundation, against which the stream beat vehemently; and immediately it fell. And the ruin of that house was great." (Luke 6:46-49)

Is your house built on the Rock? You need to be certain before the storms come. During the storm, it is too late to build a foundation. During the storm it is too late to prevent the disaster. I keep hearing the Lord say, *"It is time to restore the foundations!"* I think He is giving us an advanced prophetic word to be ready for what will soon appear. Are you personally ready for the storm? Now is the time to anchor your soul eternally in the "Rock of Ages!" If you haven't resolved that issue, do it now! Seek the Lord while He may be found! He is ready and waiting for you right now.

"For He says: 'In an acceptable time I have heard you, And in the day of salvation I have helped you.' Behold, now is the accepted time; behold, now is the day of salvation." (2 Corinthians 6:2)

Have you noticed in the Bible that the children of Israel had to rebuild the Temple foundations several times? In the days of Ezra and Nehemiah the foundation was repaired. Much later,

Herod rebuilt the Temple to appease the Jews, and it needed much foundation work. In fact, as you tour the Temple Mount, you will discover that they are still in the process of restoring the foundation. There was a major change in the amount of visible work completed between our visits in 2010 and 2011.

The problem for Israel in Biblical times was that people kept tearing it down. Several different warring nations came in and attempted to gain control by destroying their temple and getting the people to worship the false gods of the invading armies. But the truth is that Israel had already set in motion the forces to destroy the Temple by getting off the foundation of their God and going into idolatry. Temples and their foundations are always destroyed first through disobedience. When the guardian and protector of our souls is grieved and departs, the enemy is ready to move in and begin his work of destroying everything we have established for the Lord and the kingdom of God.

As I continued hearing the Lord speak about restoring foundations, a question kept coming to mind. Is it possible that the Lord is trying to warn us that we have gotten off our spiritual foundation? Every time the people of Israel set their hearts on the Lord, He restored them so they could restore the foundations. Perhaps we need to turn our hearts to God and seek His help to understand how to restore the foundations of our temple (our hearts). Our God is faithful and He is always ready to restore us and guide us in getting back on the sure foundation of faith.

> *"If My people who are called by My name will humble themselves, and pray and seek My face, and turn from their wicked ways, then I will hear from heaven, and will forgive their sin and heal their land."* (2 Chronicles 7:14)

I'VE SEEN FOUNDATIONS CRUMBLE
HOW STRONG IS YOURS?

"Therefore, leaving the discussion of the elementary principles of Christ, let us go on to perfection, not laying again <u>the foundation</u> of repentance from dead works and of faith toward God, of the doctrine of baptisms, of laying on of hands, of resurrection of the dead, and of eternal judgment. And this we will do if God permits." (Hebrews 6:1-3)

Most believers would agree that the doctrines of repentance, faith, and baptism are the foundation of the Christian faith. Not all believers agree on the purpose and place of the laying on hands, but most still accept it as foundational. Everyone seems to be able to accept the validity of the doctrine of eternal judgment. Many see it as the primary motivator for repentance and acceptance of Christ. However, a large part of the body of Christ would dispute the idea of the resurrection of the dead as a foundational doctrine. So, I ask you, the reader, "Is this a foundational doctrine for your faith?" The writer of Hebrews very clearly declares that it is part of the foundation. I have heard some argue that this is a reference to the resurrection of Jesus and the resurrection of the dead for judgment at the end of time. But they heartily disagree with the notion that it is part of the ministry of the church like all the other named doctrines in this passage.

But, consider this: If this is the foundation, and the writer says it is? Are we still founded on the resurrection of the dead? Apparently Jesus understood this as a foundational principle, and went so far as to command His disciples to raise the dead.

"Heal the sick, raise the dead, cleanse those who have leprosy, drive out demons. Freely you have received, freely give." (Matthew 10:8)

I will ask the question again. Haven't we gotten off the foundation? As I consider this passage of scripture, I am convinced that we are no longer standing on the foundation, but have somehow spent almost 2,000 years going below the standard Jesus set for his followers. I often say that we have somehow worked our way into the basement of faith rather than going from glory to glory into the very image of Jesus Christ.

How is your church group or ministry doing with these foundational doctrines? Has anyone in your church raised someone from the dead? Do you know anyone who has? According to the writer of Hebrews, this is *Christianity 101*." I believe it was so common in the time of the New Testament Church that they quit writing about it. Jesus did it! Peter did it! Paul did it! Now, everyone is doing it. It is at the foundation of who we are and what the Lord commanded us to do. Is it any wonder that the Lord keeps saying, *"It is time to restore the foundations!"*

I have heard others claim that this gift was only for the original twelve disciples. Apparently Paul didn't agree with this notion when he raised the young man from the dead who had fallen from a third story window (Acts 20). Certainly the Lord Jesus did not agree. Remember what He taught in John 14:12-14:

> *"Most assuredly, I say to you, he who believes in Me, the works that I do he will do also; and greater works than these he will do, because I go to My Father. And whatever you ask in My name, that I will do, that the Father may be glorified in the Son. If you ask anything in My name, I will do it."*

In John 17:20 Jesus says, *"I do not pray for these alone, but also for those who will believe in Me through their word;"* Both of Jesus' statements were for all those who believed in Him then and all who would believe in Him in the future. I urge you: listen to the Lord and see what He is telling you! You need a firm footing to take your stand for the Lord! I am concerned that many churches have reached the place of powerlessness in the warning Paul gave to Timothy:

> *"But know this, that in the last days perilous times will come: For men will be lovers of themselves, lovers of money, boasters, proud, blasphemers, disobedient to parents, unthankful, unholy, unloving, unforgiving, slanderers, without self-control, brutal, despisers of good, traitors, headstrong, haughty, lovers of pleasure rather than lovers of God,* **having a form of godliness but <u>denying its power</u>.** *And from such people turn away!"* (2 Timothy 3:1-5)

Are you still on the foundation established by the Lord or have you somehow gotten down in the basement with so many others who call themselves believers? What can you do if you are not on the foundation? David poses a powerful question for the church today.

> *"In the Lord I take refuge. How then can you say to me: 'Flee like a bird to your mountain.' For look, the wicked bend their bows; they set their arrows against the strings to shoot from the shadows at the upright in heart.* **When the foundations are being destroyed, what can the righteous do**?" (Psalm 11:1-3)

It doesn't have to be that way for you and me. We can embrace the teaching of Solomon in Proverbs 10:25, *"When the whirlwind passes by, the wicked is no more, But the righteous has an everlasting foundation."* As long as we are on the Lord's foundation, we will stand! Paul certainly believed this wholeheartedly and he wanted his spiritual son, Timothy, to understand it and stand on it. Read aloud what Paul taught about foundations. God's foundation will stand firm forever. The question is: Will you and I be on that foundation?

> *"Nevertheless, God's solid foundation stands firm, sealed with this inscription: 'The Lord knows those who are his,' and, 'Everyone who confesses the name of the Lord must turn away from wickedness.'"* (2 Timothy 2:19)

The Lord is saying, *"It's time to restore the foundations!"* It is time to get back in line with the Lord's plans! It is time to get back on the foundations which He established! It is time to break free from the doctrines of man which excuse us from our duty, and stand again with the Lord! Amen?

> *"Then the Lord saw it, and it displeased Him That there was no justice.* **_He saw that there was no man_**, *And wondered that there was no intercessor; Therefore His own arm brought salvation for Him; And His own righteousness, it sustained Him. For He put on righteousness as a breastplate, And a helmet of salvation on His head; He put on the garments of vengeance for clothing, And was clad with zeal as a cloak. According to their deeds, accordingly He will repay, Fury to His adversaries, Recompense to His enemies; The coastlands He will fully repay. So shall they fear The name of the Lord from the west, And His glory from the rising of the sun; When the enemy comes in, like a flood, The Spirit of the Lord will lift up a standard against him."* (Isaiah 59:1

There are supposed to be intercessor warriors called and anointed by the Lord who will step up in times of trouble, sound the alarm, and plead the case for the salvation of all mankind and the restoration of the broken down foundations. There are supposed to be intercessors willing to build a wall and stand in the gap. It is tragic when the Lord looks to and fro across the earth without finding even one.

> *"I looked for a man among them who would build up the wall and stand before me in the gap on behalf of the land so I would not have to destroy it, but I found none."* (Ezekiel 22:30)

Will the Lord find a man or woman today who will answer His call to restore foundations? Will the Lord find someone willing to step out in faith and answer the call to build that wall? Will the Lord find people who are willing to stand in the gap so that the judgment and wrath of God may be stopped so that the grace of the Lord can come to His people once again?

As I continued to study foundations, I received more revelation from the Lord. I came to see more and more clearly why the Lord is speaking to so many of us about foundations. There are so many different types of foundations and the task is too large for any one person to take on. Each of us receiving this kind of revelation has a calling from the Lord to work in one specific area. If you are one of those the Lord has called as an intercessor, I pray that you will be built up and blessed by what the Lord has revealed about the foundation He has provided for your support.

THE FOUNDATION FOR INTERCESSORY PRAYER

Then I heard the Lord say, *"It is time to restore the foundation for intercessory prayer!"* In this book, I plan to present nine of these foundation stones. I encourage you to go beyond what is written here and discover new ideas and receive greater revelations directly from the Lord.

In my study I found nine Biblical foundation stones for intercessory prayer. As I mentioned earlier, nine is the number of divine perfection and spiritual fullness. I believe that the number nine is significant and prophetic for us. However, the reality of the fullness of the blessing and the perfection of the foundation we have been given is what the Lord is declaring to be most important. Receiving the revelation of nine stones was a powerful confirmation for me that the Lord is calling us to stand on a strong and durable foundation. Throughout your study of these stones constantly ask yourself if you are firmly planted on this foundation? Are you embracing and being supported by all nine of these powerful spiritual stones? Paul also confirmed the importance of these spiritual stones for us.

> *"Moreover, brethren, I do not want you to be unaware that all our fathers were under the cloud, all passed through the sea, all were baptized into Moses in the cloud and in the sea, all ate the same spiritual food, and all drank the same spiritual drink. For they drank of that spiritual Rock that followed them, and **that Rock was Christ**."* (1 Corinthians 10:1-4)

The alternative to standing on the "Rock which was Christ" is to stand on sand with no foundation whatever. Many people in the church are not standing on the rock. I hear people talking about all of the enemy's attacks on the intercessors. There is nothing new about the enemy attacking those building foundations. We see it throughout the scriptures. What is new is that we're confessing it, and giving power to him. The Lord gave us authority over all the power of the enemy.

> *"I have given you authority to trample on snakes and scorpions and to overcome **all** the power of the enemy; nothing will harm you."* (Luke 10:19)

What part of "*all*" do we fail to understand? If you have authority over all of the power of the enemy, where is his authority to attack you, possess you, or control you? You must stand in faith and trust the words of Jesus the Christ. If He said *"all the power of the enemy"* then He meant *"all."* The same goes for the word *"nothing."* If nothing can harm us, why are we accepting this from the enemy? It is time for intercessors to stand up and continue to stand on their authority. We have been given very powerful spiritual weapons which are meant to devastate the enemy and destroy his false work in the garden of the Lord.

> *"For though we walk in the flesh, we do not war according to the flesh. For the weapons of our warfare are not carnal but mighty in God for*
>
> 1) *pulling down strongholds,*
> 2) *casting down arguments and*
> 3) *every high thing that exalts itself against the knowledge of God,*
> 4) *bringing every thought into captivity to the obedience of Christ,*
> 5) *and being ready to punish all disobedience when your obedience is fulfilled."* (2 Corinthians 10:3-6)

Are you using the Lord's weapons or relying on your own? The Lord's weapons never fail. His word never comes back void. His plans always succeed. He has already won the victory; taken the enemy's stronghold; captured his keys to the kingdom of darkness; and returned all of these to the church. It is time to stand in this authority. It's time to bring down some strongholds. It's time to bring down every high thing which exalts itself against Almighty God!

> *"For this purpose the Son of God was manifested, that He might destroy the works of the devil."* (1 John 3:8b)

Do you believe Jesus succeeded in His mission? When he shouted from the cross, "*It is finished*!" did He mean it? Was it true that He won the victory for us? If our answer is "Yes," then we need to act like it is the truth! If we are His disciples, we are to carry on His work in this world. That work is focused on destroying all the works of the devil. It is time for us to be true disciples who also destroy the works of the devil. AMEN? There is a solid foundation which is as strong today as when God established it! Are you taking your stand on the rock?

> "*So truth fails, and he who departs from evil makes himself a prey. Then the Lord saw it, and it displeased Him that there was no justice. He saw that there was no man, and wondered that there was no intercessor; Therefore His own arm brought salvation for Him; and His own righteousness, it sustained Him.*" (Isaiah 59:15-16)

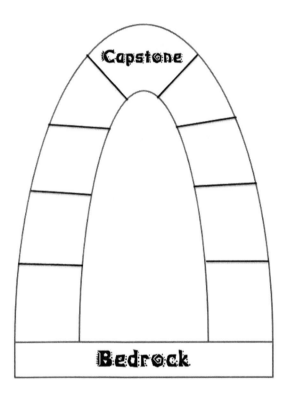

Foundation for Intercessor Warriors

CHAPTER 1

THE STONE OF AUTHORITY

❧ ❧

*D*uring that desperate season of drought in Central Texas, I came to the belief that many of the intercessors were not properly aligned with God's established system of authority. Some had gone into areas which were strongholds for the enemy and attempted to cast out principalities. According to the Bible, we can't really do that. These principalities and powers will still be present to relinquish their power to the Antichrist when he emerges. We do not have authority to do things which are not in keeping with the Word of God. Listen to what Paul taught:

> *"Finally, my brethren, be strong in the Lord and in the power of His might. Put on the whole armor of God, that you may be able to stand against the wiles of the devil. For we do not wrestle against flesh and blood, but against principalities, against powers, against the rulers of the darkness of this age, against spiritual hosts of wickedness in the heavenly places. Therefore take up the whole armor of God, that you may be able to withstand in the evil day, and having done all, to stand."* (Ephesians 6:10-13)

Paul says that we wrestle with principalities and powers. Wrestling with them outside your assigned authority can be painful and hazardous to your health. Confronting these wicked spirits in the Second Heaven is not wise. Unless the Lord specifically directs you to act against them, don't initiate a battle with them. We have been given authority to bind and to cast out the demonic spirits which come into our area of anointing and authority. We don't wrestle with them! We take authority over all their power. We should keep the teaching of Jesus stored in our hearts and be ready to use the authority He gives.

> *"The seventy–two returned with joy and said, 'Lord, even the demons submit to us in your name.' He replied, 'I saw Satan fall like lightning from heaven. I have given you authority to trample on snakes and scorpions and to overcome all the power of the enemy; nothing will harm you. However, do not rejoice that the spirits submit to you, but rejoice that your names are written in heaven.'"* (Luke 10:18-20, NIV)

For this scriptural reference, I chose the NIV translation because it uses the number 72 for those who were sent out by Jesus. These disciples were in addition to the twelve apostles He sent out earlier. The number 72 is twelve times six. When you consider this group in addition to the original twelve, you see twelve times seven. I believe this is a powerful prophetic word for us today. Twelve is the number of kingdom governance and seven is the number of spiritual fullness or spiritual perfection. I received this prophetic word to mean that Jesus was speaking to the fullness of authority given to those sent out to proclaim the gospel of the kingdom. This promise is for you and for me, and it is as powerful and effective today as it was for the disciples who were hearing Jesus that day.

Jesus had a clear understanding of the importance of authority in the kingdom. As he taught and preached, people were always amazed that He could do so with such authority. He understood clearly who He was and what God the Father had sent Him to do. His personal relationship with the Lord was the source of His confidence and the Father was the source of His authority. Jesus made this perfectly clear in the first sermon He preached.

> *"So He came to Nazareth, where He had been brought up. And as His custom was, He went into the synagogue on the Sabbath day, and stood up to read. And He was handed the book of the prophet Isaiah. And when He had opened the book, He found the place where it was written: 'The Spirit of the Lord is upon Me, Because He has anointed Me To preach the gospel to the poor; He has sent Me to heal the brokenhearted, To proclaim liberty to the captives And recovery of sight to the blind, To set at liberty those who are oppressed; To proclaim the acceptable year of the Lord.' Then He closed the book, and gave it back to the attendant and sat down. And the eyes of all who were in the synagogue were fixed on Him. And He began to say to them, 'Today this Scripture is fulfilled in your hearing.'"* (Luke 4:16-21)

Jesus understood His calling and the anointing the Lord had placed on His life. He saw how this was connected to the prophetic promises of God given centuries before. Jesus knew that He had been given authority to accomplish everything the Father had promised in the more than 300 Old Testament prophecies about the advent, life, and work of the *Messiach*. The people who heard Him preach this sermon did not know these things. They did not understand clearly. They were unprepared for what the Father was about to do through His Son, Jesus Christ.

JESUS WAS ABOUT TO CHANGE EVERYTHING THE WORLD THOUGHT IT KNEW

How do you prepare for something like that? The truth is we are not able to do it by ourselves. I remember a series of experiences, from my military career, which illustrate this truth. For many years, I attended annual training events which were called Mobilization Conferences. At these meetings, members of the army reserve and National Guard came together with active duty personnel to consider lessons learned from the previous year and to make plans for the coming year. The main purpose was to insure readiness to deal with natural and man-made disasters. Each year, we covered the lessons learned from the previous year in great detail and developed plans to prevent the same problems and failures from emerging again. At first glance, this sounds good. It was the best we knew how to do, but there was an inherent problem with this type of planning. Each year, we were planning to deal with what happened last year. As a result, we were never fully prepared for what was going to happen in the future.

One year at the conference, we dealt with how to support recovery after a major hurricane. We looked at the lessons learned and planned to do a better job in the coming year. But hurricanes were not the problem facing us. Riots broke out in a major US city and all the plans for recovering from hurricanes were of no use. At the next conference, we dealt with how to handle riots in major cities, but floods created a disaster in the heartland of America. There were no riots and the plans we made were not helpful for dealing with floods. Each year, our plans dealt with last year's challenge. You have to make plans and you need to work through lessons learned. At the same time you must understand that some things in life are not predictable. You simply cannot prepare well to handle something you do not expect and things you cannot know or understand until later.

This was the situation for those who listened to Jesus' first sermon. They simply could not understand something they had never experienced. They knew the words. They had heard the prophecies. But, somehow they had manipulated those messages to fit their world view and their religious traditions. They had been rehearsing to handle the things which had happened before. They had not received all the prophetic messages which proclaimed that God continuously does new things.

God has given us so much revelation about His future plans. Yet in many ways, we are not any better prepared than these early seekers. Many of our religious traditions are nothing more than rehearsals for things which have already happened. The doctrines and plans which have emerged from these past experiences do little to help us with what is happening now or for things which are about to happen in the future. We need to be prepared at all times for the Lord to do something completely new. We cannot know with clarity how we should deal with it, but we trust that the Holy Spirit will lead us through it if we will commit to Him. Remember what the Lord said:

"Then He who sat on the throne said, 'Behold, I make all things new.' And He said to me, 'Write, for these words are true and faithful.'" (Revelation 21:5)

To be responsive to what the Lord is doing, we have to let go of those old ways and old plans in order to embrace what God is doing in Christ right now. Many people have a strong need for structure and stability. These people are really thrown off their game when new things happen. For them this word is not good news. They may not like it, but it is the truth. The Father told John that it was true and faithful. But, you will not be left without help from the Lord as these new things happen.

Just before making this announcement to John, the Lord provided another promise:

"Then I, John, saw the holy city, New Jerusalem, coming down out of heaven from God, prepared as a bride adorned for her husband. And I heard a loud voice from heaven saying, 'Behold, the tabernacle of God is with men, and He will dwell with them, and they shall be His people. God Himself will be with them and be their God. And God will wipe away every tear from their eyes; there shall be no more death, nor sorrow, nor crying. There shall be no more pain, for the former things have passed away.'" (Revelation 21:2-4)

We need to be prepared for a time when the former things will pass away and the Lord will establish something completely new. This is not bad news as some have believed. This is good news, because we have a promise form our Father God. The new thing will be better than the old. We will not be left alone to helplessly struggle against overwhelming problems beyond our control. In the midst of change and transition, the Lord will be with us. He will literally dwell with us and in us. And when He comes to be with us, He will wipe away our tears. He will take away all our pain.

Knowing that the Lord will be with you, are you ready for something new? His promise is not just to make a few adjustments to the old system and help us to make our way through it. He has declared, that He will "make all things new." He doesn't plan to tweak the system a little here and a little there. He is going to replace it altogether. Jesus came to announce God's plans to the people. But, instead of embracing what the Lord revealed, they took offense at Jesus' words and rejected Him along with God's plans. I pray that we will do better. As you prepare yourself to adapt to these changes, think about some of the changes Jesus was announcing.

THE NATURE AND ROLE OF BIBLICAL PROPHECY CHANGED

"The law and the prophets were until John. Since that time the kingdom of God has been preached, and everyone is pressing into it." (Luke 16:16)

John was the last of the Old Testament Prophets, and Jesus was the first of the New Testament prophets. It is important to note that prophecy didn't end with John, it was changed from the time of Jesus forward. The New Testament mentions many prophets by name as well as stating that groups of prophets were traveling to visit churches. Philip the evangelist had four daughters who were prophets. In the book of Ephesians, Paul introduces the five-fold offices of ministry in the church of Jesus Christ. The second office mentioned was that of the prophet:

"And He Himself gave some to be <u>apostles</u>, some <u>prophets</u>, some <u>evangelists</u>, and some <u>pastors</u> and <u>teachers</u>, for the equipping of the saints for the work of ministry, for the edifying of the body of Christ, till we all come to the unity of the faith and of the knowledge of the Son of God, to a perfect man, to the measure of the stature of the fullness of Christ; that we should no longer be children, tossed to and fro and carried about with every wind of doctrine, by the trickery of men, in the cunning craftiness of deceitful plotting, but, speaking the truth in love, may grow up in all things into Him who is the head—Christ—from whom the whole body, joined and knit together by what every joint supplies, according to the effective working by which every part does its share, causes growth of the body for the edifying of itself in love." (Ephesians 4:11-16)

The office of the prophet is critically important to the work of the church and is essential in the building up of the body of Christ. Through the prophets, the Lord provides guidance and direction for the movement of the church. Through the work of the prophets, the Lord reveals false teaching, false teachers, and false prophets.

In addition to the office of the prophet, the Word of God points to the need for the saints to possess the "gift of prophecy." Releasing this gift is one of the ministries of the Holy Spirit in the church.

> *"There are diversities of gifts, but the same Spirit. There are differences of ministries, but the same Lord. And there are diversities of activities, but it is the same God who works all in all. But the manifestation of the Spirit is given to each one for the profit of all: for to one is given the word of wisdom through the Spirit, to another the word of knowledge through the same Spirit, to another faith by the same Spirit, to another gifts of healings by the same Spirit, to another the working of miracles, to another prophecy, to another discerning of spirits, to another different kinds of tongues, to another the interpretation of tongues. But one and the same Spirit works all these things, distributing to each one individually as He wills."* (1 Corinthians 12:4-11)

All spiritual gifts are given by the Holy Spirit in accordance with the will of God. They are given to serve a specific purpose, and only the Lord fully understands the needs of the body of Christ. Paul placed a very high value on the gift of prophecy, and urges all believers to desire this gift more than the others. He said, *"Pursue love, and desire spiritual gifts, but especially that you may prophesy."* (1 Corinthians 14:1) In 1 Corinthians 12:3, Paul gives the purpose and desired results of prophecy: *"But he who prophesies speaks edification and exhortation and comfort to men*. In more contemporary language we can understand that the gift of prophecy is given to build up, encourage, and/or comfort people. Old Testament prophets were often called on to proclaim the pending judgment and wrath of God. They pointed out the sins and failures in the lives of national leaders and the nations they served. There was very little use of prophecy to build up and bless individuals. In the New Testament, the focus shifts along with the release of the gift of prophecy. It is given to help individuals and churches to grow spiritually, overcome fear, look beyond failures, and to be comforted in times of suffering and loss.

New Testament prophecy reminds you constantly that God has a good word for you! The Father wants you to see the grace and love He has lavished on you and He wants you to know your calling and be supported in accomplishing it. So, He sends people to minister to you, to build you up, encourage you and comfort you.

To maximize your effectiveness in this season, it is important to understand that you are now living in the time of the fulfillment of Joel's prophecy.

"And it shall come to pass afterward that I will pour out My Spirit on all flesh; your sons and your daughters shall prophesy, your old men shall dream dreams, your young men shall see visions." (Joel 2:28)

Peter used this prophetic word of the Lord released through Joel to explain the behavior of the disciples on the Day of Pentecost:

"But Peter, standing up with the eleven, raised his voice and said to them, 'Men of Judea and all who dwell in Jerusalem, let this be known to you, and heed my words. For these are not drunk, as you suppose, since it is only the third hour of the day. But this is what was spoken

by the prophet Joel:' 'And it shall come to pass in the last days, says God, That I will pour out of My Spirit on all flesh; Your sons and your daughters shall prophesy, Your young men shall see visions, Your old men shall dream dreams. And on My menservants and on My maidservants I will pour out My Spirit in those days; <u>And they shall prophesy</u>.'" (Acts 2:14-18)

THE CONCEPT OF AUTHORITY WAS RADICALLY CHANGED.

"And so it was, when Jesus had ended these sayings, that the people were astonished at His teaching, for He taught them as one having authority, and not as the scribes." (Matthew 7:28-19)

When Jesus was preaching and teaching about the kingdom of God, it was the custom of rabbis to teach what other authorities from the past had said. They made comparisons and contrasted one idea or theory with another. After presenting the words of these authorities, they added their own logic and personal experiences in order to develop an understanding about the things of the Lord. They were not in an intimate relationship with the Lord and didn't receive direct revelation from Him. So, they were not able to speak with the kind of authority coming from Jesus.

"And when the Sabbath had come, He began to teach in the synagogue. And many hearing Him were astonished, saying, 'Where did this Man get these things? And what wisdom is this which is given to Him, that such mighty works are performed by His hands! Is this not the carpenter, the Son of Mary, and brother of James, Joses, Judas, and Simon? And are not His sisters here with us?' So they were offended at Him." (Mark 6:2-3)

Some were offended by Jesus' authority. (Mark 6:3b, *"So they were offended at Him."*) Because they didn't understand, they took offense at Him, His methods, and His teachings. These individuals were unable to receive the good news of the gospel of the kingdom of God. They were unable to receive the deep revelation Jesus brought into the mysteries of God. Their inability to understand, and their unwillingness to receive the Truth blocked them from receiving their healing, miracles, signs and wonders. Remember what Mark wrote about the gifts and blessings they missed.

"Now He could do no mighty work there, except that He laid His hands on a few sick people and healed them. And He marveled because of their unbelief. Then He went about the villages in a circuit, teaching." (Mark 6:5-6)

Many people today are also offended by Jesus' authority. An unbelieving world has once again rejected His teachings. We are usually able to see this clearly and point to national failures, but the problem actually goes much deeper than this. Many in the church reject Jesus' authority, and even more reject the idea that He gave authority to those who are led by the Holy Spirit. Many theologians and church leaders are teaching with no authority of their own or with any claim to Jesus' authority. If people receive and accept these powerless teachings, they deprive themselves of the faith that brings the power of God to His people. The results are the same today as in the time Jesus was preaching and teaching. A lack of faith still limits the work of God, and He will do no miracles in their midst and only a few will receive healing. The Lord, Jesus made it clear that the world does not see the truth, because it cannot see or know the Spirit of truth. The world simply cannot receive it.

"And I will pray the Father, and He will give you another Helper, that He may abide with you forever—the Spirit of truth, whom the world cannot receive, because it neither sees Him nor knows Him;" (John 14:16-17a)

The German philosopher, Friedrich Hegel (1770-1831) once said, *"The only thing we learn from history is that we learn nothing from history."* This maxim seems to be true in much of the church today. Even though this account of Jesus' ministry is read Sunday after Sunday, the lessons are not truly learned by many church leaders, because they limit its message to that time and that situation. We need to do better than this.

We need to be careful that we do not make the same mistake today. We need to seek understanding and revelation about the authority God has given to those who follow Him. If you don't know how to do that, ask the Holy Spirit! It is part of His mission. Remember what Jesus said,

"I still have many things to say to you, but you cannot bear them now. However, when He, the Spirit of truth, has come, <u>He will guide you into all truth</u>; for He will not speak on His own authority, but whatever He hears He will speak; and He will tell you things to come. He will glorify Me, for He will take of what is Mine and declare it to you." (John 16:12-14)

If immature believers cannot understand or receive the deep things of God, then the world is certainly at a loss to grasp these revelations from the Lord. Tragically, unbelief can cause you to miss the hour of your visitation. Jesus wept over people who were unable to see and receive the things they so desperately needed.

"Now as He drew near, He saw the city and wept over it, saying, 'If you had known, even you, especially in

this your day, the things that make for your peace! But now they are hidden from your eyes. For days will come upon you when your enemies will build an embankment around you, surround you and close you in on every side, and level you, and your children within you, to the ground; and they will not leave in you one stone upon another, because you did not know the time of your visitation.'" (Luke 19:41-44)

As disciples of Jesus Christ, we should also feel the sadness of Jesus over the lost children who could not receive the good news of the gospel of the kingdom of God. I pray that we will not miss the time of our visitation! I pray that we will not let the doctrines of man prevent us from seeing the truth of God! I pray that we will not fail to see and operate in the authority the Lord has given us!

IN ADDITION TO CHANGES IN PROPHECY AND AUTHORITY ALL PREVIOUS COVENANTS WERE MADE NEW AND COMPLETE

Through the work of Jesus Christ, the sacrificial law was fulfilled, and the Lord offered a new covenant: a covenant of grace. We do not have to make atonement for our sins over and over. We don't have to make sacrifices over and over. We don't need to shed the blood of lambs, bulls, goats, or birds. The Lord has done everything for us that is needed to satisfy the requirement of the law.

"But this Man, after He had offered one sacrifice for sins forever, sat down at the right hand of God, from that time waiting till His enemies are made His footstool. For by one offering He has perfected forever those who are being sanctified." (Hebrews 10:12-14)

The covenants in the Feasts of the Lord were changed. Some believe the feasts have been abolished, but this is not scriptural. The feasts will still be celebrated during the millennial reign of Jesus Christ. The feasts of the Lord give us an opportunity to remember what the Lord has done for us and give Him the glory, honor, praise, and thanksgiving He so richly deserves. The last three feasts of the Lord are a prophetic acting out of the second coming of the Lord and serve as a reminder and rehearsal for the things to come. These feasts increase our level of understand of the times, seasons, and promises of the Lord. He commanded that these should be celebrated throughout all generations, and I want to remain faithful and obedient to His word. At the same time, we remember that the sacrificial law has been fulfilled. The sacrificial elements of this covenant of the feasts has been changed and fulfilled through the work of Jesus Christ. We no longer practice the sacrificial portions of the feasts, but recognize Jesus as the fulfillment of all of these requirements. The covenant has changed, and the promises of God are even greater than in the past.

Jesus changed the Passover celebration forever by instituting the Lord's Supper during His last Passover Seder on the earth. He did not say to stop celebrating Passover. He said to remember Him as we eat and drink during the celebration. I love to celebrate Passover because it enhances my understanding of what Jesus said and did on that last night with the disciples. I don't think we can understand it fully apart from the Seder meal. Everything in that meal pointed to the coming of the Messiah. Everything in that meal is today a celebration of the faithfulness of God to fulfill His promises and deliver us from our slavery to sin, death, hell, and the grave! With every celebration of the Passover, my love and gratitude toward the Lord God grows stronger and deeper! It is my joy to remember and lift up my praise and thanksgiving to Father God.

The covenant of blessing the Lord made with Abraham has also changed. It has been expanded to include all the nations on earth. This was God's plan from the beginning, but somehow got lost over time.

> *"Now the Lord had said to Abram: 'Get out of your country, From your family And from your father's house, To a land that I will show you. I will make you a great nation; I will bless you And make your name great; And you shall be a blessing. I will bless those who bless you, And I will curse him who curses you; And in you all the families of the earth shall be blessed.'"* (Genesis 12:1-3)

Through the work of Jesus Christ, the gentiles (the nations) have been grafted into the olive tree. The Lord expanded the reaches of the covenant to include you and me. Thanks be to God that He has done this for us through the person and work of Jesus Christ!

> *"And if some of the branches were broken off, and you, being a wild olive tree, were grafted in among them, and with them became a partaker of the root and fatness of the olive tree, do not boast against the branches. But if you do boast, remember that you do not support the root, but the root supports you. You will say then, 'Branches were broken off that I might be grafted in.' Well said. Because of unbelief they were broken off, and you stand by faith. Do not be haughty, but fear."* (Romans 11:17-20)

Through the work of Jesus, Father God grafted us into the covenant made with Abraham thousands of years ago. This opened the door of blessing for every child of God on the planet. This work of God in Jesus Christ made it possible for us to receive all the blessings of Abraham and the Jewish people. Through Abraham and earlier through Noah the Lord was returning kingdom authority to His people. In Jesus Christ,

He made the fullness and depth of this promise clear to all who would follow Him.

> *"Christ has redeemed us from the curse of the law, having become a curse for us (for it is written, 'Cursed is everyone who hangs on a tree'), that the blessing of Abraham might come upon the Gentiles in Christ Jesus, that we might receive the promise of the Spirit through faith."* (Galatians 3:13-14)

Remember that the *"promise of the Spirit"* had to do with receiving power and authority. After His resurrection from the dead, Jesus told the disciples to go to Jerusalem and wait for the promise of God to be fulfilled. They were to receive power when the Holy Spirit came upon them. Power comes to the place where authority has already been established. This power and authority are still available to believers today. It is available to all who are led by the Holy Spirit. Remember the prayer of Jesus recorded in John 17:18-23:

> *"As You sent Me into the world, I also have sent them into the world. And for their sakes I sanctify Myself, that they also may be sanctified by the truth. I do not pray for these alone, but also for those who ᵗwill believe in Me through their word; that they all may be one, as You, Father, are in Me, and I in You; that they also may be one in Us, that the world may believe that You sent Me. And the glory which You gave Me I have given them, that they may be one just as We are one: I in them, and You in Me; that they may be made perfect in one, and that the world may know that You have sent Me, and have loved them as You have loved Me."*

WHY AREN'T WE LIVING IT NOW?

What happened? Where did the authority and power go? Why are so few living at this level of authority today? I believe that it is partially because we've spent most of the last 2,000 years rebuilding religious traditions similar to the ones which limited people who were being taught by Jesus. In the Garden of Eden, Adam and Eve committed high treason and gave their power and authority to the serpent. Each generation since that time has made the same mistake. We have born the image of the man and woman of dust, but it is not to be that way any longer.

"And as we have borne the image of the man of dust, we shall also bear the image of the heavenly Man." (1 Corinthians 15:49)

The fall of man in the garden resulted in all mankind being tempted to walk in the image of the man of dust. Apart from God, this is all that is possible in the natural. Beginning with the first citizens of earth, the natural image took the front seat, and they began to live in and for the flesh.

The divine image was cast aside because it was not valued in accordance with God's Word. It was then forgotten by many people throughout the centuries. From time to time, God acted in dramatic ways to reestablish kingdom authority in the people of His creation. Remember what the Lord said to Noah after the flood:

"So God blessed Noah and his sons, and said to them: 'Be fruitful and multiply, and fill the earth. And the fear of you and the dread of you shall be on every beast of the earth, on every bird of the air, on all that move on the earth, and on all the fish of the sea. They are given into your hand.'" (Genesis 9:1-2)

Over time, people once again lapsed back into a powerless life focused on the flesh. Over and over people failed to live up to the image which God had given to them in the creation. In the days of Moses, people had given their authority and power to Pharaoh, Egypt, and the many idols of the people. So much was given up that the nation had been reduced to slavery and hard labor. Yet, when they cried out to Father God, He sent a deliverer who not only led them out of captivity, but also operated in the power and authority God had given to humanity. In the beginning, the staff of Moses was the symbol of that authority.

"Then the LORD said to Moses, 'Why are you crying out to me? Tell the Israelites to move on. Raise your staff and stretch out your hand over the sea to divide the water so that the Israelites can go through the sea on dry ground.'" (Exodus 14:15-16, NIV)

Of course, the power belonged to God, but the authority was given to Moses. When Moses moved in the authority given to him by God, the power came with it. Can you imagine the Lord speaking to you this way? Can you imagine Him telling you to lift your staff and part the sea? Probably not! And that is the problem. We can only walk in as much authority as our faith can carry. We have lived too long under the influence of the spirit of religion. Remember that the root meaning of the word religion is binding. It was given so that we could bind ourselves to Father God in a loving personal relationship. When we fail to establish this relationship, we are vulnerable to the spirit of religion.

It is the objective of the spirit of religion to bind you so that you cannot freely respond to what God is doing in the present time. The spirit of religion works to get us focused on issues of words, ideas, and doctrines while we ignore the power and authority. This spirit wants us to believe that we are doing a good thing when we sit around arguing instead of taking a stand to change the world through the gospel of Jesus Christ. We need to be clear about which spirit is leading us. Is it a spirit of religion or is it the Holy Spirit of God?

Don't forget the enemy's plan! Remember what Jesus said about the enemy in John 10:10a, *"The thief does not come except to steal, and to kill, and to destroy."* The enemy wants to steal your authority, power, blessing, and favor from God. He wants to kill your hopes and dreams. Then he plans to destroy your influence and work in the kingdom of God. But, Jesus came with a very different purpose. Listen to what He says about Himself in John 10:10b, *"I have come that they may have life, and that they may have it more abundantly."*

In Christ, our relationship with God has been transformed. Our God given image has been restored. In other words, the image of the heavenly man was restored to us. For some people, this is difficult to receive. They have lived under the influence of a spirit of poverty for so long that it is difficult to envision living in the blessing, favor, prosperity, power, and authority of God. They have come to believe that this image is false and represents a spirit of pride.

People have been taught a false humility which convinces them to live in denial of who they are in Christ Jesus. As long as we give the Lord all the glory and attribute all the credit to Him, it is not pride. There is a false pride which embraces a low self-image in order to feel holy and righteous. Anything which does not speak to God's truth is part of the lie. People who are oppressed by this false spirit of humility — which is actually low self-esteem — simply don't accept the changes inherent in this restoration. This is not only false pride, but more tragically it is rebellion against God.

When we embrace who we are in Christ and live in the fullness of what that means, we are living in Biblical humility. Living up to the image of God, puts us back into a position of authority. In this position, the blessing of Adam, Noah, and

Abraham are our text books. We are called to walk in the same authority and to release the same power which characterized their work for the Lord. This is not from human pride. It means that we are using the authority He has given to accomplish our mission.

Remember that what the Lord gives, He gives to keep our part of the garden working in accordance with His plan. Embracing and living in the image of God puts us back into a position of dominion. Jesus restored to us our dominion over the power of the enemy.

"Behold, I give you the authority to trample on serpents and scorpions, and over all the power of the enemy, and nothing shall by any means hurt you." (Luke 10:19)

At times, people in the church behave as if Christ has not defeated Satan. However, the truth is that Christ came to restore us to kingdom authority. Part of this means that we are to take up the call of God and fulfill His command to:

"Be fruitful and multiply; fill the earth and subdue it; have dominion over the fish of the sea, over the birds of the air, and over every living thing that moves on the earth." (Genesis 1:28)

Jesus boldly proclaimed that He has given us authority over all the power of the enemy. What part of "all" are we having difficulty understanding. James, the brother of Jesus and pastor of the church in Jerusalem, reveals to us the way to get the devil out of our area of operation.

"Therefore submit to God. Resist the devil and he will flee from you. Draw near to God and He will draw near to you. Cleanse your hands, you sinners; and purify your hearts, you double-minded." (James 4:7-8)

It's time to deal with the enemy as Father God prophesied to the serpent in Genesis 3:15,

"And I will put enmity between you and the woman, And between your seed and her Seed; He shall bruise your head, And you shall bruise His heel."

It is time for us to kick snake and take names! Ultimately this speaks to the role of Jesus as the "seed" of the woman. Jesus came to destroy the works of the devil. In 1 John 3:8b, the apostle John describes Jesus' **_purpose_**: *"For this purpose the Son of God was manifested, that He might destroy the works of the devil."* As disciples of Jesus, we carry on His mission. If it was His purpose to destroy the works of the devil, we take up the same cause and work faithfully to accomplish the same mission.

At this point, I would like to pause and make some decrees. I invite you to make the same decrees. I invite you to speak them aloud. We learn at a deeper level what we speak with our own mouths. As the mouth speaks the heart receives. It is also important to remember that faith comes by hearing. Say forcefully with me:

1. Father God, You have made me a new creation!
2. I decree that I have been made new!
3. I have been recreated in your image!
4. Jesus came to set us free, and I am free indeed!
5. I accept the authority you have given to me!
6. I will walk, talk, and minister in this authority!
7. Along with Jesus, I will destroy the works of the devil!
8. I am a person of authority!
9. I will do what Father God calls me to do, in Jesus Name! Amen!!!
10. These decrees are not about guilt; present of past.

11. I will not let the enemy lead me into a trap of shame, judgment or condemnation about failing to walk in this authority in my past!
12. I decree that I am released from the enemy's influence over my life!
13. I am proclaiming and embracing the restoration needed to walk in His authority!
14. I want to receive everything Jesus paid for on the cross, including kingdom authority!

Do you want to receive what Jesus paid for on the cross? Do you want to be free from the oppression of a spirit of religion? Would you like to operate in kingdom authority accompanied by the power of God? Then begin to study and embrace the powerful Word of God available to you. Read aloud, receive in your heart, and always remember the powerful words Paul gave to the Colossian church:

"Having disarmed principalities and powers, He made a public spectacle of them, triumphing over them in it." (Colossians 2:15)

GOD IS RAISING UP
A NEW GENERATION OF WARRIORS

"Who may ascend into the hill of the Lord? Or who may stand in His holy place? He who has clean hands and a pure heart, who has not lifted up his soul to an idol, nor sworn deceitfully. He shall receive blessing from the Lord, And righteousness from the God of his salvation. This is Jacob, the generation of those who seek Him, Who seek Your face." (Psalm 24:3-6)

I believe that we are called to be *a generation* that seeks and finds the Lord's face. Adam, Abraham, and Moses walked and talked with God face to face. Each one of them had an intimate relationship with the Lord. Out of this relationship and the close association with the Lord, they began to reflect His glory and His attributes. They began to operate more and more in His authority as He released it to them. If we want to walk with the Lord and begin to operate in this kind of kingdom authority, we must desire the face of God more than anything else. It is time to press in to our position at His side. It is time to become the men and women God created us to be.

I don't know about you, but I am a warrior. God called me to be a warrior! In every aspect of the ministry He has given to me, I see myself as a warrior. This is not always a comfortable position. Don't expect to always be comfortable and to receive comforting words. The Lord woke me up at 3:00 in the morning. I sat up in bed, instantly made wide awake. Then I heard the audible voice of the Lord say, *"From the foundation of the world, the enemy determined to destroy you!"* I took that personally. Several thoughts went through my mind. I said, *"How dare he make such a decision! What did I ever do to him to cause this to happen?"*

Obviously, it was not something I had done, that resulted in him making the decision to destroy me thousands of years before I was born. As I thought about this word from the Lord, I started to understand many other promises of God. I knew at a personal level that this ancient enemy made this decision about each of us. He made this same murderous decision about you. He wants to kill you after he has robbed you. He wants to destroy everything you have been called to do for the kingdom of God. He has made a declaration of war against all the saints of God! Sitting up in bed at 3:00 a.m., I made a decision of my own. If it is war he wants, then it is war he will have. I made some decrees in the wee hours of the morning. I spoke a paraphrase of some old American rhetoric used by many sources: *"I will not go quietly or gently into the night! I will not give up without a "life and death" fight! I will live eternally with my*

Lord Jesus Christ! If you kill me, I will come back with Him to rule and reign on earth for a thousand years! With God's help, I will be the warrior He has called me to be! Amen and Amen!!!!!" War has been declared and warriors have been called up for active duty. Are you a warrior? Have you heard the call? How will you respond? Are you ready for battle?

> *"Proclaim this among the nations: 'Prepare for war! Wake up the mighty men, let all the men of war draw near, let them come up. Beat your plowshares into swords and your pruning hooks into spears; Let the weak say, '"I am strong.""* (Joel 3:9-10)

In this age, we are in a season where we can see wimps becoming warriors. In addition to hearing the weak proclaiming their strength, I am seeing spineless people decreeing and receiving a back bone. Please pardon the directness of these words, but I think the time for gentleness, political correctness and apathy is over. We are in a life and death struggle to determine whether we have the right to exist on this earth. I have heard the battle cry and the call of God to war. I am seeing people in increasing numbers hearing the battle cry and responding to the call.

The mighty men and women of God are lining up to go to war along with Him. This is the generation to see the warring champions re-emerge. These warriors are like the dreaded champions of David's army. These are the mighty champions who like the sons of Issachar *"understand the times and know"* what God's people should do. For this generation and for this season of war, the Lord is releasing to His people His mighty spiritual weapons of warfare.

> *"For though we walk in the flesh, we do not war according to the flesh. For the weapons of our warfare are not carnal but mighty in God for pulling down*

strongholds, casting down arguments and every high thing that exalts itself against the knowledge of God, bringing every thought into captivity to the obedience of Christ, and being ready to punish all disobedience when your obedience is fulfilled." (2 Corinthians 10:3-6)

I trust God and I trust His promises. God always stands by His word and always keeps His promises.

Our loving and faithful Father God does not give kingdom authority and then capriciously take it away. After His death and resurrection, Jesus received all authority on heaven and earth. Then, He passed the kingdom authority for this world back to us and promised that He and his authority will be with us until the end of the age.

"And Jesus came and spoke to them, saying, 'All authority has been given to Me in heaven and on earth. Go therefore and make disciples of all the nations, baptizing them in the name of the Father and of the Son and of the Holy Spirit, teaching them to observe all things that I have commanded you; and lo, I am with you always, even to the end of the age.' Amen." (Matthew 28:18-20)

I have been asked, "Why doesn't God just come down and fix everything Himself?" In a vision from the Lord, I looked up and saw heaven open with Jesus standing in the opening. I cried out, *"Jesus, please come down and fix things for us!"* I heard a resounding, *"No!"* Then Jesus said, *"I have already done that! Now it is up to you! You fix things!"* This is not cold or callous. It is the truth. I ask you to remember Psalm 115:16, *"The heaven, even the heavens, are the Lord's; But the earth He has given to the children of men."*

If we believe the Word of God (and I do), then we understand that the Lord has given authority to you and me to subdue, have dominion over, and manage our part of His garden on earth. We have the same call as Adam and Noah. We also have the same command from the Lord.

> *"Then God blessed them, and God said to them, 'Be fruitful and multiply; fill the earth and subdue it; have dominion over the fish of the sea, over the birds of the air, and over every living thing that moves on the earth.'"* (Genesis 1:28)

God gave us the earth and the task of having dominion over it. He gave us the authority to subdue it. Jesus restored everything lost in the Garden of Eden and returned that authority to us. Our just and righteous Father God does not take this lightly. He waits for our permission to enter the battle. He waits for us to step out on faith. He waits for us to bring His power into our area of authority. He waits for us to raise the staff of authority and part the sea of sin, doubt, and tribulation.

Fully trained intercessor warriors know how to open the door to let Him and His power come into our area of operation. God has more than enough power and greater forces than needed to defeat the enemy. So, what is He waiting for? He is waiting for us to commission Him and release our authority back to Him.

EFFECTIVE INTERCESSORS KNOW THEIR AUTHORITY

> *"Then He called His twelve disciples together and gave them power and authority over all demons, and to cure diseases. He sent them to preach the kingdom of God and to heal the sick."* (Luke 9:1-2)

How you intercede in prayer is driven by how you see your authority. This is one of the reasons it is so important for intercessors to know their authority. Do you know your kingdom authority? Remember that you can ask the Holy Spirit for guidance. He has come to guide you into all truth and this is an important part of God's truth. Once you come to know your level of kingdom authority, your prayers will change. You will be enabled to pray with command authority in your area of responsibility. You will come to understand that you can pray with the authority delegated to you by others in their area of responsibility. It is also important to know that as a member in the Kingdom of God, you can pray with the authority of a member or citizen.

I wonder how many people know the primary source of this authority. We must be acutely aware that all kingdom authority comes to us from the Father through Jesus Christ. Most believers embrace the Great Commission as it is given in the gospel of Matthew. Most can agree that Jesus is speaking the truth of God when He says that all authority in heaven and on earth has been given to Him. However, many believers miss the point of Jesus delegating that authority to His disciples then and now. Immediately after proclaiming His authority, He points to his disciples and releases that authority to them. They will need it to accomplish the huge mission ahead of them. Study again the full impact of this commission. As you read it aloud this time, receive it as His commission given directly to you.

> *"And Jesus came and spoke to them (me), saying, 'All authority has been given to Me in heaven and on earth. (I give part of my authority to you so that you can) Go therefore and make disciples of all the nations, baptizing them in the name of the Father and of the Son and of the Holy Spirit, teaching them to observe all things that I have commanded you; and lo, I am with you always, even to the end of the age.' Amen."* (Matthew 28:18-20)

Do you believe that Jesus was speaking truthfully when He said that He has been given "*all authority*?" Do you really believe this? If you do, then how much authority on earth is left over for the devil and his demonic forces? If you believe that Jesus has it all, then there is nothing left for the enemy.

In the last days, when the Antichrist has been made manifest and is in power, authority will be given to him, the false prophet, and the dragon. But, we are not in that time yet. So, what is the source of the enemy's authority? I believe the answer is made clear in the Revelation of John. Consider the two passages below:

"So they worshiped the dragon who gave authority to the beast; and they worshiped the beast, saying, 'Who is like the beast? Who is able to make war with him?'" (Revelation 13:4)

"The ten horns which you saw are ten kings who have received no kingdom as yet, but they receive authority for one hour as kings with the beast. These are of one mind, and they will give their power and authority to the beast." (Revelation 17:12-13)

In the last days, during the time of the great tribulation, people and leaders will give their authority to these enemy forces. But that time has not yet arrived. The problem is that many people (including many believers) have prematurely given their authority to the enemy. This should not happen! Even in the great tribulation, there is nothing to say that believers will give up their authority. Only those who are following the Antichrist will give up their authority. For now, we stand on the authority Jesus has given. Remember in Luke 10:19, Jesus states that he has given us authority over all the power of the enemy. Paul was certainly aware of this when he instructed his disciple, Titus, *"Speak these things, exhort, and rebuke with all authority. Let no one despise you."* (Titus 2:15)

If you are operating in your assigned area of authority, the Lord gives you the power to accomplish His purposes in your life and ministry. The head of a household has spiritual authority over the whole family. The person exercising this authority must understand that this does not cancel the authority the Lord gives to his/her family members in their assigned mission areas. Spouses and children have authority in their own areas of responsibility. It is the authority to stand with or against the enemy. Believers must continue to stand against the enemy and all his works. It is your assignment to keep divine order in the mission field given to you by the Lord.

I also recommend that you go through a personal Biblical study of the concept of divine order. Have you noticed the word "order" comes up over and over in the description of the Tabernacle and the Temple? Everything had to be placed in order and everything had to be done in the proper order. Through the setup and operation of these two places of worship, the Lord was making a principle very clear. He is not a God of disorder! *"For God is not a God of disorder but of peace."* (1 Corinthians 14:33, NIV)

David learned this lesson the hard way when he decided to move the Ark of the Covenant to Jerusalem. He didn't consider God's commands about the proper order for moving the ark. He did it the way the Philistines had done it. The death of one of the helpers was the result of dishonoring God by handling His sacred things out of order. Listen to David's own words:

> *"And David called for Zadok and Abiathar the priests, and for the Levites: for Uriel, Asaiah, Joel, Shemaiah, Eliel, and Amminadab. He said to them, 'You are the heads of the fathers' houses of the Levites; sanctify yourselves, you and your brethren, that you may bring up the ark of the Lord God of Israel to the place I have*

prepared for it. For because you did not do it the first time, the Lord our God broke out against us, because we did not consult Him about the proper order.'" (1 Chronicles 15:11-13)

Everything in the Kingdom of God is orderly and established in the *"proper order!"* This also goes for the lines of spiritual authority. These lines of authority are clearly delineated in God's Word. It is critically important to understand this as you go through this lesson. Also remember that we're talking about spiritual authority. I recommend that you pause and reflect on who has spiritual authority over you? Then consider those over whom you have spiritual authority. Ask yourself, "What authority has the Lord released directly to me?"

The unfortunate truth is that people, including some who call themselves believers, constantly choose to rebel against many of God's lines of authority. Some Christians reject the authority of their pastors. Families rebel against the lines of authority God set up. Liberated wives sometimes rebel against the spiritual authority of their husbands. Children rebel against their parents, and students rebel against the authority of their teachers. Have you noticed that in both families and church families where God's authority is rejected the result is disunity, distress, disharmony, disappointment, and dysfunction? The truth is that if we want things to work for the good of all, we have to do it God's way.

In the midst of all this rebellion, the enemy has an easy time disrupting the working of the church. When intercessors fail to see their authority, they tend to allow the enemy to work against them. In their testimonies about all the things the enemy is doing to them, they relinquish their spiritual authority back to him. This is not their intention, but it is the result of failing to recognize and operate in the authority God has given to them.

It is time for intercessors to step out in their God given authority and pray down enemy strongholds, break off all enemy oppression, and strip him of all the authority he has received in error. Remember the promises of the Bible. What can the enemy do to you? Some people act as if this is some kind of great struggle we are doomed to lose. This is completely unbiblical. Stand on the powerful promise of James 4:7, *"Therefore submit to God. Resist the devil and he will flee from you."* Only two things are needed to put the devil on the run and neither of them will cause you to work up a sweat. Just submit to God and resist the devil. That's all it takes. Believe it! Receive it! Stand on it! And, do it! Amen?

GOD'S TRUE WARRIORS
ARE THE INTERCESSORS

"And you, being dead in your trespasses and the uncircumcision of your flesh, He has made alive together with Him, having forgiven you all trespasses, having wiped out the handwriting of requirements that was against us, which was contrary to us. And He has taken it out of the way, having nailed it to the cross. Having disarmed principalities and powers, He made a public spectacle of them, triumphing over them in it." (Colossians 2:13-15)

True intercessors stand on the authority given to them by God through the redeeming work of Jesus Christ. They know that the enemy has been disarmed. Principalities and powers have been stripped of all their weapons of warfare. The Lord made a public spectacle of them on the cross. It is time for the true intercessor warriors to arise. The alarm has sounded, and the Lord has called for his mighty men and women to assemble. It is time to bring down strongholds and defeat every argument of the enemy.

We have listened to and prayed too many wimpy prayers. God is not calling wimps. He is calling warriors. Warriors hear the sound of battle and then rush to join the fight. They don't beg and whine. They fight with the power and authority God has given to them.

We need to drop the whiny prayers that beg God for help. If it's in the Word and in your authority, **pray like it**. Take a stand on faith, the Word, God's power, and your authority. Speak authoritative decrees in the mighty name of Jesus Christ! Release the kind of power in prayer that will bring down every argument against the Lord, His kingdom, and His people!

Don't ask Jesus to come down and fix things. Remember: I tried that once. The Lord said to me with great authority, *"No! I have already done that! Now, it is your turn to fix things! Use the authority I gave you and get the job done!"* This is one of those moments when disciples (like good soldiers) snap to attention, salute and say *"Yes Sir!"* This is the Biblical response. Remember what Paul wrote to the believers in Roman:

> *"But the righteousness of faith speaks in this way, 'Do not say in your heart, "'Who will ascend into heaven?'"' (that is, to bring Christ down from above) or, "'Who will descend into the abyss?'"' (that is, to bring Christ up from the dead). But what does it say? 'The word is near you, in your mouth and in your heart' (that is, the word of faith which we preach):"* (Romans 10:6-8)

Always remember that Jesus has already done His part, and He sealed it when He proclaimed on the cross, "It is finished!" Pause for a moment and think about the full meaning of Hebrews 1:13: *"But to which of the angels has He ever said: 'Sit at My right hand, till I make Your enemies Your footstool'"*? The correct answer is that this word was given only to Jesus. Jesus completed His work, and is now seated next to God resting until His enemies are made into His footstool. The writer of Hebrews wanted to make this point very clear and very strong. So, he wrote about it again:

"But this Man, after He had offered one sacrifice for sins forever, sat down at the right hand of God, from that time waiting till His enemies are made His footstool." (Hebrews 10:12-13)

Jesus clearly understood His mission, His authority, His responsibility, and His power. He operated at the level of His anointing, and used the power and authority Father God had given Him to do His work. Then Jesus turned to us and tasked us to do the same thing He had done. We must remember whose work we are called to do. Ultimately it is all about doing the will and work of Father God on the earth.

"For I have come down from heaven, not to do My own will, but the will of Him who sent Me." (John 6:38)

For the ongoing work of the Kingdom of God on the earth, Jesus left the authority, responsibility and ability with us. I realize that many of you haven't been taught like this in the past. Many of us have grown up still praying children's prayers. Why do you need to learn about this now? It is because now the battle lines have been drawn. War has been declared, and we are called to the battle. To succeed and keep the victory Jesus won, we have to do it God's way.

"Proclaim this among the nations: 'Prepare for war! Wake up the mighty men, let all the men of war draw near, let them come up. Beat your plowshares into swords and your pruning hooks into spears; Let the weak say, "'I am strong."'" (Joel 3:9-10)

We often refer to people who hear this word and take up the fight as Joel's Army. If you count yourself among these warriors, then recognize that you have been called to active duty. Are you part of this army of the Lord? Are you ready to suit up and show up? Are you ready to stand on the foundation stone of authority and complete the work you have been called to do?

I have heard too many people making excuses and quoting the words of an old hymn. "*Gentle Jesus, meek and mild, look upon a little child.*" (Charles Wesley, "*Gentle Jesus, meek and mild,*" Classic Poems for Children. (Public Domain)) Those who quote this old song often take it out of context to justify a fruitless life of fear and defeat. As sweet as these old words may sound, they are a poor description of the Jesus I know from the Word of God. In these passive words, there is no concept of the triumphant Son of God, Who entered the domain of death, hell and the grave, and emerged victorious. This little nursery rhyme says nothing about the powerful warrior King, Jesus Christ, who entered the strongman's house and took the power of death from him.

Today, we need prayers that proclaim the mighty Son of God Who took Satan captive; broke his power; bound him in chains; and proclaimed liberty to a world crushed and bound by the fear of the power of death. We need new prayers, new hymns, and new courage to stand. We stand today against a defeated enemy. Our task is to cast him out, forever. Be courageous! Do not fear! God's power is with you. Remember and embrace the words of Paul in Romans 8:37: "*Yet in all these things we are more than conquerors through Him who loved us.*"

People make up all kinds of excuses to justify what I will bluntly call "cowardly behavior." They misquote the scriptures, make up rationalizations, and promote fear in others. My friends this should not be happening. We must tell the truth of God in love so that His people will not be deceived. There is no place for the cowardly in the kingdom of God. According to the Bible, the first people to go into the lake of fire will be the cowardly. Listen to what the Lord said to John:

"He who overcomes shall inherit all things, and I will be his God and he shall be My son. But the cowardly, unbelieving, abominable, murderers, sexually immoral, sorcerers, idolaters, and all liars shall have their part in the lake which burns with fire and brimstone, which is the second death." (Revelation 21:7-8)

METHOD USED TO ILLUSTRATE STANDING ON THE FOUNDATION STONES

As I moved from writing about restoring foundations to teaching before live audiences, I looked for dramatic ways to illustrate these principles. It seemed very natural to act it out by taking a physical step with my left foot onto the stone which represents kingdom authority. Then I stepped with my right foot onto the second stone in the foundation. There is something powerful about acting out a prophetic word. The Lord always puts something into the equation when His people step out in faith. So, I asked people in the training conferences to stand up and begin to claim the promises by stepping out, standing on the stones, and stepping into the authority and power God put into each stone. People responded positively to this suggestion and had fun stepping on the stones in order to claim the Biblical promises that they could go higher and higher in kingdom authority.

My recommendation to you as a reader is to do the same thing. Don't worry about what other people may see or think. You don't want to be among the cowardly anyway! I like to step firmly on the stones to reflect the power and commitment I am putting behind my decision to stand on the principles God has given to me in His Word.

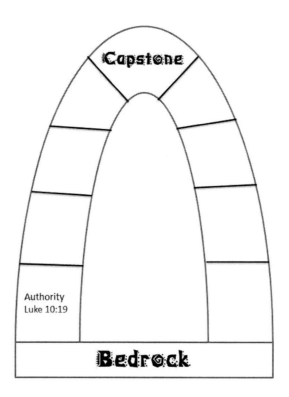

Authority: The First Stone of the Foundation

EXERCISE

TO INCREASE YOUR BIBLICAL FOUNDATION

Read the passages of scripture below and make notes on how these Biblical verses help to increase your understanding of authority as a foundation stone for those who are intercessor warriors.

"And whatever you ask in My name, that I will do, that the Father may be glorified in the Son. If you ask anything in My name, I will do it." (John 14:13-14)

1.

2.

3.

"No longer do I call you servants, for a servant does not know what his master is doing; but I have called you friends, for all things that I heard from My Father I have made known to you. You did not choose Me, but I chose you and appointed you that you should go and bear fruit, and that your fruit should remain, that whatever you ask the Father in My name He may give you." (John 15:15-16)

1.

2.

3.

"And in that day you will ask Me nothing. Most assuredly, I say to you, whatever you ask the Father in My name He will give you. Until now you have asked nothing in My name. Ask, and you will receive, that your joy may be full." (John 16:23-24)

1.

2.

3.

"Assuredly, I say to you, whatever you bind on earth will be bound in heaven, and whatever you loose on earth will be loosed in heaven. 'Again I say to you that if two of you agree on earth concerning anything that they ask, it will be done for them by My Father in heaven. For where two or three are gathered together in My name, I am there in the midst of them.'" (Matthew 18:18-20)

1.

2.

3.

"So I sought for a man among them who would make a wall, and stand in the gap before Me on behalf of the land, that I should not destroy it; but I found no one." (Ezekiel 22:30)

1.

2.

3.

"Therefore I exhort first of all that supplications, prayers, intercessions, and giving of thanks be made for all men, for kings and all who are in authority, that we may lead a quiet and peaceable life in all godliness and reverence. For this is good and acceptable in the sight of God our Savior," (1 Timothy 2:1-3)

1.

2.

3.

CHAPTER 2

THE STONE OF THE WORD

"For no other foundation can anyone lay than that which is laid, which is Jesus Christ. Now if anyone builds on this foundation with gold, silver, precious stones, wood, hay, straw, each one's work will become clear; for the Day will declare it, because it will be revealed by fire; and the fire will test each one's work, of what sort it is. If anyone's work which he has built on it endures, he will receive a reward. If anyone's work is burned, he will suffer loss; but he himself will be saved, yet so as through fire." (1 Corinthians 3:11-15)

With your left foot firmly established on the authority God has given you, its time to step up on the next foundation stone. Place your right foot firmly on the stone called the "Word of God." There are at least three different aspects to the Word of God as we are using it here. First, the Bible refers to the authority and power released through the spoken Word of God. By this word, the universe came into being. By this word everything is still established. The Word of God was spoken through His prophets long before it was written down on paper.

Next, scripture makes reference to the written Word of God which we receive in and through our Bibles. Jesus used this word to deal with the temptations of the devil. *"But Jesus answered him, saying, 'It is written, 'Man shall not live by bread alone, but by every word of God.'"* (Luke 4:4) Paul points his spiritual son, Timothy, to the written word of God as the source which will guide him and equip him for the work of the gospel.

"All Scripture is given by inspiration of God, and is profitable for doctrine, for reproof, for correction, for instruction in righteousness, that the man of God may be complete, thoroughly equipped for every good work." (2 Timothy 3:16-17)

Finally, the Bible refers to the living Word of God (Hebrews 4:12a, *"For the word of God is living and powerful"*) How can the word be alive? It is alive because it is embodied in our Lord Jesus Christ. He did much more than merely speak the written Word of God. He is the living Word of God.

"He was clothed with a robe dipped in blood, and His name is called The Word of God." (Revelation 19:13)

Peter attests to this fact and adds that the Word of God will live forever. We can be assured of that, because Jesus the Christ will live forever. He was raised from the dead as the first fruits of all who would be raised to eternal life.

"Since you have purified your souls in obeying the truth through the Spirit in sincere love of the brethren, love one another fervently with a pure heart, having been born again, not of corruptible seed but incorruptible, through the word of God which lives and abides forever," (1 Peter 1:22-23)

Are you standing on a sure foundation? Are you standing on the foundation stone of the Word of God? If you are an intercessor, you must stand on this stone as the solid rock which holds all the rest of your spiritual house up. You must stand on the Word of God in order to firmly establish your prayers of intercession on a solid foundation. If you are an intercessor warrior, this foundation stone is absolutely essential as a position on which you are to take your stand and continue to stand. We stand on this same stone which Jesus used in dealing with the devil and all his attempts at deception. This foundation stone is our proof that God is with us and our assurance of His abiding presence even to the end of time. Reflect back on Paul's advice to Timothy. Scripture is the means the Lord uses to make us *"complete, thoroughly equipped for every good work."*

GOD EQUIPS AND TRAINS
HIS INTERCESSORS WARRIORS

We will begin with a short review of the teaching in the first chapter. I do this for two reasons. First, many people don't begin to read at the beginning, and this will help orient them to where we are with our understanding of foundations for intercessor warriors. And, secondly, it is good to deepen your learning through repetition of key concepts. David often spoke of meditating on God's Word. The words he used referred to learning by saying something over and over. I continue to encourage you to read the scriptural references aloud. This is a powerful learning technique which Paul recommended to the church in Rome.

"How then shall they call on Him in whom they have not believed? And how shall they believe in Him of whom they have not heard? And how shall they hear without a preacher? And how shall they preach unless they are sent? As it is written: 'How beautiful are the feet of

those who ^f*preach the gospel of peace, Who bring glad tidings of good things!' But they have not all obeyed the gospel. For Isaiah says, 'Lord, who has believed our report?' So then <u>faith comes by hearing</u>, and <u>hearing by the word of God</u>.*" (Romans 10:14-17)

In the previous chapter, we demonstrated that God gives authority and dominion to His people. This was not a new idea coming with the advent of Jesus. It was God's plan from the beginning of His creation.

"The heaven, even the heavens, are the Lord's; but the earth He has given to the children of men." (Psalm 115:16)

The Lord's plan was short circuited by Adam and Eve in the Garden of Eden when they relinquished their authority to the serpent. God did not let their failure stop Him from accomplishing His plan and His purpose for mankind. He re-established His plan with Noah, Abraham, David, and etc. In each case, He took the authority back from the enemy and returned it to these individuals and the people they represented. Each of these men was given authority to subdue the world around them and to exercise dominion over it. They were to pass this authority along to those who followed them. However, their descendants made the original mistake of Adam and Eve over and over again.

The ultimate revelation of this was in Jesus the Christ who took authority back from Satan and returned it to us. We are to hold on to this victory and never again give our authority to the enemy. It is important to note that Jesus clarified the extent of this victory. He clearly stated that He had received all authority in heaven and on the earth.

"And Jesus came and spoke to them, saying, 'All authority has been given to Me in heaven and on earth. Go therefore and make disciples of all the nations, baptizing them in the name of the Father and of the Son and of the Holy Spirit, teaching them to observe all things that I have commanded you; and lo, I am with you always, even to the end of the age.' Amen." (Matthew 28:18-20)

It is good to know that we have authority. At the same time, we need to know the extent and limitations of our God given authority.

1. You do not now nor will you ever have authority over God.
2. You have authority over what is yours — over your territory.
3. You have authority over all the power of the enemy in your assigned area.

"Behold, I give you the authority to trample on serpents and scorpions, and over all the power of the enemy, and nothing shall by any means hurt you." (Luke 10:19)

Intercessor Warriors learn to pray with authority! They understand that they have been given command authority over the works of the devil in their personal lives, their families, and in their ministries. They also have limited authority in their extended family, church, school, or work place. Using your spiritual authority in prayer does not mean that you are telling God what to do. You are telling the enemy what to do and where to go. You can use it to kick the devil out. You don't need to fight with him or wrestle with him when you are exercising the authority you have been given to complete the mission the Lord has assigned to you. You don't have to work or strive to accomplish it. Remember James 4:7, *"Therefore submit to God. Resist the devil and he will flee from you."*

Many people have a difficult time accepting their spiritual authority and operating with it, because they have created a hole in their hedge of protection. I have found four primary sources for holes in the hedge. These four things which make you open and vulnerable to an enemy attack are willful disobedience, fear, rebellion, and sin. If you find the enemy operating in your area, kick him out. Then close the hole in the hedge and get focused again on Jesus. Praying James 4:7 is a good way of getting the enemy out of your area. Then find the hole and close it.

If the hole is disobedience, get back into obedience. You begin by recognizing and acknowledging your disobedience. Then confess it to the Lord, and ask for His forgiveness. He is faithful and just to forgive our sin. He will forgive all sincerely confessed disobedience. Then make a plan to stay in obedience. You may need to make some personal changes in your lifestyle or environment. You may need to get rid of things which tempt you and avoid people who lead you astray. You can ask the Lord for help. This is one of the primary functions of the Holy Spirit. Remember, He has been sent to guide you into all truth.

If the hole in your hedge of protection is fear, you have the authority to cast out a spirit of fear remembering what Paul said in 2 Timothy 1:7, *"For God has not given us a spirit of fear, but of power and of love and of a sound mind."* When you cast this spirit out, remember to fill the empty space so it has no room to return. The Bible tells us what will best fill this space. Fill it with God's perfect love.

"Love has been perfected among us in this: that we may have boldness in the day of judgment; because as He is, so are we in this world. There is no fear in love; but perfect love casts out fear, because fear involves torment.

93

But he who fears has not been made perfect in love." (1
John 4:17-18)

If the hole in your protective covering is a result of some
degree of rebellion against the Lord or any of His established
lines of authority, acknowledge it and ask the Lord for His forgiveness. Once again ask the Holy Spirit to come to you as
a power source of wisdom and revelation to give you a full
understanding of what you need to do to align yourself with
the Lord and restore the authority and power He has given to
you as a disciple of Jesus Christ. Hebrews 3:7-8, *"Therefore,
as the Holy Spirit says: 'Today, if you will hear His voice, do
not harden your hearts as in the rebellion, In the day of trial in
the wilderness'"*

If the hole in your hedge of protection is sin, repent and
return to an obedient life with the Lord. Remember 1 John
1:8-9, *"If we say that we have no sin, we deceive ourselves, and
the truth is not in us. If we confess our sins, He is faithful and
just to forgive us our sins and to cleanse us from all unrigh-
teousness."*

After you have reestablished the integrity of your covering,
get back into the blessing of Abraham. Start operating again
with your God given authority.

Authority is just one of the stones in the foundation of an
intercessor warrior. Your God given authority defines your
territory and the Lord releases His power along with your
authority to do His work. When you begin to operate in your
God given authority, you need to take up the armor of God and
use your weapons for spiritual warfare.

Your primary weapon for spiritual warfare is the sword of
the Spirit. As you study the passage below from the book of
Ephesians, I want you to notice two very specific things about
what Paul is saying. First, and most easily seen, is that the
sword of the Spirit is the Word of God. However, the second
part of this is often overlooked. This message is specifically for

those who are interceding for the saints. This word is targeted toward helping intercessor warrior.

"And take the helmet of salvation, and the sword of the Spirit, which is the word of God; praying always with all prayer and supplication in the Spirit, being watchful to this end with all perseverance and supplication for all the saints" (Ephesians 6:17-18)

WE MUST STAND ON THE WORD OF GOD

I have heard many times in the past that the *"sword of the Spirit"* is the only offensive weapon Paul identifies with the armor of God. However, after studying this closely for several years I have come to disagree with this statement. I believe that interceding and praying in the Spirit are also offensive weapons. These mighty spiritual weapons release the awesome power of God to bring down strongholds along with every argument and exalted thing established against the knowledge of the Lord. These are the spiritual weapons which are able to bring thoughts into captivity and into obedience to Christ.

"For though we walk in the flesh, we do not war according to the flesh. For the weapons of our warfare are not carnal but mighty in God for pulling down strongholds, casting down arguments and every high thing that exalts itself against the knowledge of God, bringing every thought into captivity to the obedience of Christ, and being ready to punish all disobedience when your obedience is fulfilled." (2 Corinthians 10:3-6)

Praying in the Spirit along with the Word of God (the Sword of the Spirit) are the only spiritual weapons we will ever need to overcome the enemy and cast him out of our area of operations. With prayer and the Word, we can overcome every work of the devil.

No wise soldier goes into battle unarmed. Many believers do not want to hear this. They sincerely believe that if they compromise with the world they can live in peace. These people deny the reality of our current spiritual warfare. Too many churches want peace at any cost. Make no mistake, we are at war. We didn't start it. The enemy made the first move. He declared war and launched a full scale attack on the saints of God. The battle will go on whether you like it or not. When the enemy declares war you no longer have an option for peace. You either stand up and fight or go silently into the darkness and death of night. It is time for the body of Christ to wake up from sleep and follow the leadership of our conquering King.

Long ago, the prophet Joel brought a powerful word from the Lord. It is time to wake up! We all need to wake up; especially the mighty warriors of the Lord's army. If you are called to be an intercessor warrior, it is time to wake up and prepare for battle. Read the prophecy aloud once more, and hear it as your call to active duty.

> *"Proclaim this among the nations: 'Prepare for war! Wake up the mighty men, let all the men of war draw near, let them come up. Beat your plowshares into swords and your pruning hooks into spears; Let the weak say, 'I am strong.'"* (Joel 3:9-10)

The Word of the Lord provides all the material we need to make our own swords and spears. Many people make the mistake of waiting for the Lord to take charge and hand them a sword. They don't plan to move until the Lord points them toward the enemy. The message of the Lord is for us to get some of our own weapons in addition to the sword He provides. Do you believe that the Lord is truly asking us to make swords in the natural to go with the one He gives in the spiritual? Apparently that is exactly what He is saying. Consider what Jesus said to the disciples:

> *"Then He said to them, 'But now, he who has a money bag, let him take it, and likewise a knapsack; and he who has no <u>sword</u>, let him sell his garment and <u>buy one</u>.'"* (Luke 22:36)

We do not fully understand what the Lord is telling us. In Luke 22:38, we see how the disciples answered, "*Lord, look, here are two swords.*" And He said to them, "*It is enough.*" The message seemed clear at this point, but the disciples must have been confused by Jesus' response when Peter actually used the sword.

> *"And suddenly, one of those who were with Jesus stretched out his hand and drew his sword, struck the servant of the high priest, and cut off his ear. But Jesus said to him, 'Put your sword in its place, for all who take the sword will perish by the sword. Or do you think that I cannot now pray to My Father, and He will provide Me with more than twelve legions of angels?'"* (Matthew 26:51-53)

Have you struggled with these apparent inconsistencies in the Word? I asked the Lord to give me understanding, and this is what I received. The answer to the apparent confusion is found in the original message of the Load through Joel. The Lord said that we should convert the tools we have learned to use for seedtime and harvest into weapons of war. These are tools for planting the seeds of the Word of God in our hearts and into the hearts of those we teach and mentor. These are tools for planting seeds of faith into the lives of others. These are tools for planting financial seeds in kingdom futures. These are spiritual weapons also because they are advancing the kingdom of God and bringing down enemy strongholds in our lives and in the lives of those we are reaching for Jesus Christ. I believe that there is also some value to having a physical sword. It is meant to serves as a prophetic act of stepping into an anointing of the Lord. We are not to actually fight with this sword at this time. But we do apparently need to take some action which will activate the Biblical promises for spiritual weapons to be given and received.

We need the wisdom of God to fully understand these things. We need the wisdom of ". . .*the sons of Issachar who had understanding of the times, to know what Israel ought to do. . .*" (1 Chronicles 12:32) Wise men and women who are disciples of Jesus Christ know the times and what the Lord's people should be doing. These wise servants know in the Spirit when it's time to convert their harvesting tools into weapons of war.

The wise servants go to God in intercessory prayer in season. They are prepared for God's next move of the Spirit. They have taken up the sword of the Lord rather than the weapons of earthly warfare and understand that these are more powerful than all the weapons of the enemy. They know that what they actually have is the mighty Word of God which never comes back void, and is never overcome by the enemy.

This weapon of the Word of God will overcome the power of the devil for you in the same way it worked for Jesus when the enemy came to Him after His wilderness experience. Jesus was obviously physically tired, thirsty, and hungry. His physical strength may have been at a low point after forty days of fasting, but the Word of God was as powerful as ever. It did not fail Him and it will not fail you! Jesus took up the "sword of the Spirit' and defeated every argument Satan could raise up against the Lord. Jesus was a skilled swordsman who expertly used His spiritual sword. He was then and is still now a mighty man of war. We need to remember who Jesus really is and understand that He will return with this same sword to conquer and rule.

"He was clothed with a robe dipped in blood, and His name is called The Word of God. And the armies in heaven, clothed in fine linen, white and clean, followed Him on white horses. Now out of His mouth goes a sharp sword, that with it He should strike the nations."
(Revelation 19:13-15)

Jesus is the Word of God, and He uses the Word to conquer. With the Word of God He defeated in the past. With the Word of God, Jesus is defeating the enemy in the present, and He will defeat him again in the final battle at the end of time. And, with the Word of God (this mighty sword) He will defeat the nations. Those who stand with Him have the victory now and it is theirs for all eternity.

Meditate on this powerful message from the Lord. He accomplishes all these things with the Word of God. Let your faith rise higher and higher. Come to know and believe with absolute certainty that this is the same sword He places in your hands, now.

We have the sword of the Spirit now, and we need to be using it right now. I have heard some people say, "I'm waiting to receive that power when I get to heaven." This is not the message given by the Lord. We are at war now and we need the power of God in order to hold on to the victory Jesus won for us. Consider this: You won't need authority and weapons in heaven. Satan won't be there. There will be no causes to fight for or battles to be won. Now is the time for us to take up the sword of the Lord and accomplish His mission and purpose for our lives and for the kingdom of God. True spiritual sons and daughters of Issachar know that now is the time to stand and fight.

GOD'S WORD IS SHARPER THAN A TWO-EDGED SWORD

"For the word of God is living and powerful, and sharper than any two-edged sword, piercing even to the division of soul and spirit, and of joints and marrow, and is a discerner of the thoughts and intents of the heart." (Hebrews 4:12)

Real power is not with the armies in our world or with manmade weapons. God is our source and He has ultimate and eternal power. We need to shift our focus from the world to the Word. In your hand, the sword of the Lord is more powerful than nuclear weapons. Like David, you need to let the Lord teach you how to fight. You need to let Him train you and strengthen you to the point you can make the same affirmation as David: *"He teaches my hands to make war, so that my arms can bend a bow of bronze."* (2 Samuel 22:35)

The sword of the Lord pierces to the division of the soul and spirit. This means that it gets right at the heart of our situation. There is a great battle taking place right now for your soul. The Lord has claimed it, but the enemy comes with lies and deception in order to steal it for himself. Every temptation of the enemy is an attempt to destroy your soul and your effectiveness for the kingdom of God. When disciples fall into sin they give a victory to the enemy. We know from the Word of God that there is a war raging inside each one of us. When we give in to the enemy and let him lure us into immorality and sin, we are rejecting what Jesus did for us. This should not be. The Lord won that victory at a great price — his own blood.

"Beloved, I beg you as sojourners and pilgrims, abstain from fleshly lusts which war against the soul," (1 Peter 2:11)

If we store the Word of God in our hearts as Jesus did, we will be prepared to handle every enemy attack. There is a passage of scripture for every temptation and trial brought on by the devil. Some comedians imitate old time preachers by saying sarcastically, *"It's in the book!"* In spite of their attempt to make it a joke, this is actually true. It is in the book, and the book is the "sword of the Spirit." As the writer of Hebrews 4:12 tells us, we can use this sword to separate out and remove everything that is not of the kingdom of God. It is better to do that now rather than wait for the final judgment. Paul gives the same advice.

> *"But in accordance with your hardness and your impenitent heart you are treasuring up for yourself wrath in the day of wrath and revelation of the righteous judgment of God, who 'will render to each one according to his deeds': eternal life to those who by patient continuance in doing good seek for glory, honor, and immortality; but to those who are self-seeking and do not obey the truth, but obey unrighteousness—indignation and wrath, tribulation and anguish, on every soul of man who does evil, of the Jew first and also of the Greek; but glory, honor, and peace to everyone who works what is good, to the Jew first and also to the Greek."* (Romans 2:5-10)

With this mighty weapon of the Word of God we purify our hearts. As we read in the book of Hebrews, the sword divides the soul and the spirit. Like marrow in a bone, the spirit is encapsulated in the soul. Marrow nourishes, purifies, and protects the blood in our physical bodies. That is a good thing. When the body is under attack by a bone cancer, the marrow is the first place it causes damage. In its natural state it can no longer fight the good fight. It needs to get out of the bone, be cleansed and purified and then returned to the bone in order to conquer cancerous diseases. This illustrates the work of the sword of the Spirit in dividing our soul and spirit so that the spirit can be born again. Then the new creation in us begins to transform the soul through the renewing of our minds. For this reason, this passage from chapter four of the book of Hebrews tells us that the Word of God (the sword) discerns the thoughts and intents of the heart.

> *"Then Simeon blessed them, and said to Mary His mother, 'Behold, this Child is destined for the fall and rising of many in Israel, and for a sign which will be spoken against (yes, a sword will pierce through your own soul also), that the thoughts of many hearts may be revealed.'"* (Luke 2:34-35)

The things which are to be revealed by the "sword of the Spirit" are the things which in the natural we don't want out in the open. However they must be dealt with for us to be renewed in our minds in order to experience the transformation of our souls. If unresolved, these things in our minds will hold us back, and retard the process of our spiritual development. This will continue to be a problem until we let the Holy Spirit purge them with His mighty sword. It is the Word of God stored in our hearts which serves as the source of discernment in the spiritual realm. This spiritual discernment reveals the parts of our soul still somewhat bound to the flesh.

A SCARY WEAPON —
HEAVY AND DIFFICULT TO USE

Even though in the natural world the sword is a weapon of fear, we are not to fear it. The Lord does not give us a spirit of fear. When you feel fear, remember the source. It comes from the enemy. It does not come from the Lord. When you feel fear, speak the Word of God in order to restore your faith.

There are two scriptures I recommend that you memorize and use regularly. Say them over and over right now! Repeat them until your faith builds up into real spiritual power. Continue to speak them aloud until all fear is gone!

"So then faith comes by hearing, and hearing by the word of God." (Romans 10:17)

"For God has not given us a spirit of fear, but of power and of love and of a sound mind." (2 Timothy 1:7)

If faith comes by hearing the Word of God, where does fear come from? I believe that it also comes by hearing. It comes by hearing the word of the enemy. Stop listening to him! When you are tempted, go to the Word and speak it over your situation and put the enemy on the run.

GOD TRAINS US TO USE THE WEAPONS OF WAR

Remember the story in the first book of Samuel about David fleeing from King Saul. Since he had to escape so quickly to save his life, he didn't stop to take provisions for the journey or weapons for protection. The only place he knew he could go for help was to the Tabernacle of the Lord. There He met with, Ahimelech, the priest and asked for food and weapons.

"So the priest said, 'The sword of Goliath the Philistine, whom you killed in the Valley of Elah, there it is, wrapped in a cloth behind the ephod. If you will take that, take it. For there is no other except that one here.' And David said, 'There is none like it; give it to me.'" (1 Samuel 21:9)

When David defeated Goliath the giant, he took his sword as a prize. However, it was too heavy for him to handle. So, he left it in the Tabernacle of the Lord. David was a shepherd at that time and not a trained soldier. The sword was probably too heavy for most of Israel's trained warriors as well. It belonged to a giant and was made to be compatible with a giant's size and strength. At that time, David was not even able to use Saul's armor and sword. Several things had changed since that victory over the giant. In the intervening years, David had been trained to use a sword and had fought in many battles. Like the other warriors in Israel, the sword of Goliath should have been too big and too heavy for David even with his training and practice. However, he was now prepared to use this powerful weapon. What changed? David allowed God to train him and strengthen him. David proclaimed:

"Blessed be the Lord my Rock, who trains my hands for war, and my fingers for battle. . ." (Psalm 144:1)

With God's training, David was ready to take up the sword of Goliath. How about you? Are you ready to take up the sword of the Spirit? Remember: this is your time for training and preparation. Now is time to get your sword sharpened, oiled, and ready. Now is the time for building up your strength and developing your skill by practicing daily with the sword. After your training and with the anointing of the Lord, you will be able to say with David:

"He teaches my hands to make war, so that my arms can bend a bow of bronze." (Psalm 18:34)

The ideal is to get trained and ready before the battle begins, but we don't have that luxury. The war started before we were born. When we were brought into the world, we were also brought into the battle. All of your life, you have lived in a war zone, and it is time to act like you are aware of the times. It is never too late to get the Word of God activated in your life. However, it is critically important for intercessor warriors to have this worked out now in order to have the results God desires from your prayers and supplications for all the saints.

In this very hour, we are enmeshed in the greatest battle of human history. We are warring for the very souls of men and women around the world. We are warring for our right to exist on this planet. The stakes are high and we cannot afford to lose even one battle. We should already be fully prepared for the battle. By now, we should have the Word in our hearts. By now, we should be fully trained by the Spirit. Unfortunately, not all of the Lord's intercessors can truthfully say they are ready. I am not writing this to bring shame and condemnation on anyone. I am writing these things because it is time to wake up, prepare yourselves, and remain ready in faithful obedience to the Lord, Jesus Christ. It is time to choose sides and take your stand. May the words in the passage below never be a true description of even one of the Lord's anointed intercessors!

"For though by this time you ought to be teachers, you need someone to teach you again the first principles of the oracles of God; and you have come to need milk and not solid food. For everyone who partakes only of milk is unskilled in the word of righteousness, for he is a babe. But solid food belongs to those who are of full age, that is, those who by reason of use have their senses exercised to discern both good and evil." (Hebrews 5:12-14)

It's tragic that so many of the Lord's disciples are unprepared for war. There really is no adequate excuse. The message was made clear centuries ago. We have heard the messages, listened to the sermons, attended classes, and received revelation knowledge from the Lord. What excuse could we possibly make? May we all heed the call of the Lord repeated throughout the scriptures and get busy making every preparation for the battle as we develop our combat skills. Remember: gifts and skills are strengthened by reason of use. This is the meat of the Word. This is the solid food we should be receiving daily from the Lord.

> *"But solid food belongs to those who are of full age, that is, those who by reason of use have their senses exercised to discern both good and evil."* (Hebrews 5:14)

One of the old-time Christmas carols asks a critical question: "Do you see what I see?" I want to ask that question of you now. Do you see what I see? Do you see what John saw before he wrote the book of Revelation?

> *"And I saw thrones, and they sat on them, and judgment was committed to them. Then I saw the souls of those who had been beheaded for their witness to Jesus and for the word of God, who had not worshiped the beast or his image, and had not received his mark on their foreheads or on their hands. And they lived and reigned with Christ for a thousand years."* (Revelation 20:4)

SWORDS ARE USED TO CONFER TITLES AND POSITIONS

In the past, Kings and queens used swords to confer knighthood on brave warriors who had proven their leadership, courage and skills on the battlefield. Today, they do it to give prestigious honors to people in appreciation for their work in the nation. Often, no bravery or combat experience is needed to receive the honor of knighthood. Entertainers, celebrities, and musicians are sometimes given recognition with these titles.

In times gone by, Swords were used to convey titles during ceremonial services of consecration. During times of war, swords may be used to assign a position to one of the king's valiant knights. Along with the titles came great responsibilities. Those wishing to receive the titles had to be willing to give oaths of loyalty and dedication. They were required to take these oaths in order to affirm their willingness to meet all the requirements of the office and accept the responsibilities assigned to them.

God has chosen to uses His Word (sword) to convey titles and positions. In days gone by, the Lord spoke through His prophets to notify people of their selection as kings and prophets. Many of the kings of enemy nations had their titles and positions conferred on them by God's Word through His prophets. Look carefully at two representative scriptures below:

"Then the Lord said to him: 'Go, return on your way to the Wilderness of Damascus; and when you arrive, anoint Hazael as king over Syria.'" (1 Kings 19:16)

"As they were going down to the outskirts of the city, Samuel said to Saul, 'Tell the servant to go on ahead of us.' And he went on. 'But you stand here awhile, that I may announce to you the word of God.'" (1 Samuel 9:27)

In the Word of God, we learn who Christ was, who He now is, and who we are in Him. Long ago the prophets of God gave a detailed description of the role, function, purpose, and appearance of the Messiah King. When Jesus arrived on the scene, He fit all these descriptions and fulfilled all the prophetic words given centuries before.

In the Word, we learn about who we are as kingdom citizens serving under the Lordship of Jesus the Christ. We discover in the written Word and through the spoken Word of the Holy Spirit about our authority, our dominion, and our area of responsibility. It is also in the Word that we discover the extent and limitations of that authority God has conferred on us.

It is critically important for you to understand that the sword of the Lord does no good on a shelf or hanging on the wall as an ornament. Too many people put their titles on display rather than living them out. In the military, we called a wall filled with certificates, plaques, and awards an "ego wall." We all know people who have all the certificates and diplomas, but, have no idea what to do with their training or how to occupy their assigned positions. To be effective as intercessor warriors you must take up the sword daily and stand up for the Lord. If you lack wisdom in these areas, just ask the Lord. He is faithful and He will give you what you need to succeed. Father God is the only source of true spiritual wisdom. You can ask and receive it from Him, but you have to pray in faith. Without faith nothing will be fully conferred to you.

"If any of you lacks wisdom, let him ask of God, who gives to all liberally and without reproach, and it will be given to him. But let him ask in faith, with no doubting, for he who doubts is like a wave of the sea driven and tossed by the wind. For let not that man suppose that he will receive anything from the Lord; he is a double-minded man, unstable in all his ways." (James 1:5-8)

God is faithful to provide what we need to accomplish His purpose. He is a good Father who lavishes gifts and wisdom on His children. Trust Him to accomplish what He set out to do in you. Have faith that He will provide for you. Believe that what you ask of Him in prayer you will receive by faith. Too many people ask, but let doubt steal their blessings. If you are double-minded, don't expect your prayers to be answered. Begin to read the scriptures which assure you that God will keep His promises. Store them in your heart for later use. Repeat them over and over until faith builds to the point of releasing the power. God is the sole source for wisdom and it is no mystery about how you are to receive it.

"If you then, being evil, know how to give good gifts to your children, how much more will your heavenly Father give the Holy Spirit to those who ask Him!" (Luke 11:13)

Whatever you do, don't go into battle against a deadly enemy unarmed, untrained, or unprepared. Remember it is never too late to get started. Begin right now to appropriate the weapons, the training, and the wisdom to use them. Make a fresh commitment to God today, then take up the "sword of the Spirit," and use it as God intended. If you ask the Lord, he will help you get stronger every day.

HOW DO INTERCESSOR WARRIORS APPLY THE WORD?

1. PRAY WHAT IS ALREADY IN THE WORD

You can be certain that there is nothing false in the Word of God. In John 17:17 we see where Jesus said, *"Sanctify them by Your truth. Your word is truth."* The testimony of Jesus is that the Word of God is truth. You can trust the words of Jesus and you can trust the Word of God. If God said it, He will do it! Listen to what the Psalmist had to say about God's Word:

"The entirety of Your word is truth, And every one of Your righteous judgments endures forever." (Psalm 119:160)

When you pray the Word of God, you are praying the truth. You are praying what God has already said. You are praying for things which have already been established. You are praying for things in agreement with the Lord. Listen to the affirmation given by Paul in Romans 3:4, *"Indeed, let God be true but every man a liar."* Trust the Word of God over the words of man every time.

The first step is to become intentional about praying the Word of God. Before you begin to intercede ask yourself if what you are asking can be found in the Word of God. If not, don't pray for it. Have you ever attended a prayer group where this was practiced? Most intercessory groups just jump in and start praying what they believe is needed without consulting the Word of God.

2. PRAY BIBLICAL PRAYERS

Begin to study some of the great prayers in the Bible. Most of us have studied the "Lord's Prayer" and know it by heart. However, I don't think we have yet squeezed out of that prayer everything that Jesus intended to provide for us when He taught it to the disciples. Don't stop here, with just the "Lord's Prayer" without digging deeper into the Word! Look at some of the prayers given by the apostles. A representative sample can be found below:

"Therefore I also, after I heard of your faith in the Lord Jesus and your love for all the saints, do not cease to give thanks for you, making mention of you in my prayers: that the God of our Lord Jesus Christ, the Father of glory, may give to you the spirit of wisdom and revelation in the knowledge of Him, the eyes of your understanding being enlightened; that you may know what is the hope of His calling, what are the riches of the glory of His inheritance in the saints, and what is the exceeding greatness of His power toward us who believe, according to the working of His mighty power which He worked in Christ when He raised Him from

the dead and seated Him at His right hand in the heavenly places, far above all principality and power and might and dominion, and every name that is named, not only in this age but also in that which is to come." (Ephesians 1:15-21)

How would you like for someone to consistently pray this over you, your church, and your ministry? Just imagine all these gifts of God flowing into your life as a result of this prayer. Think for a moment about the authority and power God would release to you because the saints have prayed this over you! Wow! I would certainly like for someone to pray for me this way. Here is another great example of a powerful Biblical Prayer:

"For this reason I bow my knees to the Father of our Lord Jesus Christ, from whom the whole family in heaven and earth is named, that He would grant you, according to the riches of His glory, to be strengthened with might through His Spirit in the inner man, that Christ may dwell in your hearts through faith; that you, being rooted and grounded in love, may be able to comprehend with all the saints what is the width and length and depth and height—to know the love of Christ which passes knowledge; that you may be filled with all the fullness of God. Now to Him who is able to do exceedingly abundantly above all that we ask or think, according to the power that works in us, to Him be glory in the church by Christ Jesus to all generations, forever and ever. Amen." (Ephesians 3:14-21)

This prayer by the Apostle Paul is another great prayer I would like for others to pray over me. How about you? Try to imagine what the Lord can do with a prayer like this. Imagine the Lord providing for you according all the riches of His glory.

Wow! Think about being strengthened in your inner being by the power of the Holy Spirit so that Christ could literally live in you all the time. What would it mean for you, your family, and the church if you were rooted and grounded in the kind of love Jesus has for you? What would you receive if the Lord provided exceedingly and abundantly more than you have ever asked or imagined? Study this prayer and see what other benefits you might draw out from it and pray it into your life and over the lives of those you love and serve.

Here is one more example of a powerful prayer which you can pray over your own life and ministry by paraphrasing it to put it into the first person:

> *"And this I pray, that your love may abound still more and more in knowledge and all discernment, that you may approve the things that are excellent, that you may be sincere and without offense till the day of Christ, being filled with the fruits of righteousness which are by Jesus Christ, to the glory and praise of God."* (Philippians 1:9-11)

Don't stop with these examples. Find other prayers which you can incorporate into your intercessory prayers for the saints. Because these prayers are in the Word of God, there is great power and authority available through these prayers. When you pray these prayers you are in agreement with the Lord, the Holy Spirit, and the apostles who wrote and prayed them. As you get into agreement with Father God and all the saints of the past, think about how much power you will release. You can trust these prayers and the power of God behind them. You can rightly expect supernatural results every time you pray the Word of God. Remember that *"Every word of God is pure; He is a shield to those who put their trust in Him."* (Proverbs 30:5)

Place your foot firmly on the foundation stone of God's word. If you are standing with Him you will never be shaken.

If you are standing on His Word, you may have confidence that He will accomplish His purpose as stated in His Word. He does not contradict Himself or go back on His word. Nothing He speaks will come back void. When the Lord speaks, things happen. At the Word of the Lord, things are created, thinks are restored, things are made new, and things are made manifest. The world was created by His Word and everything in it is sustained by His Word. Once you learn to pray this way, you will release great power through your prayers.

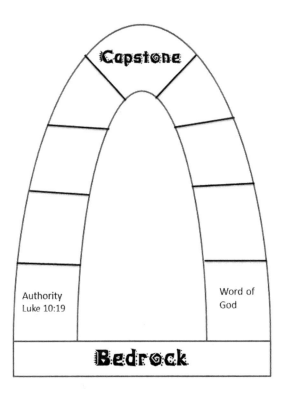

Word of God — The Second Stone in the Foundation

CHAPTER 3

THE STONE OF AGREEMENT

ဗၩ‍ဒၩ

"But at midnight Paul and Silas were praying and singing hymns to God, and the prisoners were listening to them. Suddenly there was a great earthquake, so that the foundations of the prison were shaken; and immediately all the doors were opened and everyone's chains were loosed." (Acts 16:25-26)

A good foundation can take a great deal of shaking without breaking. The Lord shook the foundations of the prison to set Paul and Silas free. I believe this passage is more than just an historical account of the work of the apostles; although that would be enough to bless us. When I read passages of scripture like this, I am inspired and begin to rejoice that the Lord safeguarded Paul and others so that their work could be completed and handed down through time to me. These events recorded in scripture minister to us and strengthen our faith. Yet, I believe there is more to the message than just these things. I always ask the Holy Spirit for wisdom and revelation to understand the Word of God more fully. As I prayed, the Lord spoke to my spirit to help me understand more fully what I should receive from this account now.

Sometimes the Lord needs to do some shaking of our foundations to set us free from the things which bind us and oppress us. I welcome His shaking, because He always brings about something new and better. At the same time, I am aware that there are some foundations which must never be shaken. For example:

"For no other foundation can anyone lay than that which is laid, which is Jesus Christ." (1 Corinthians 3:11)

This is one foundation the Lord will never allow to be shaken or broken. Your perspective on and understanding of this foundation may need to be shaken from time to time, but the Lord will never allow the foundation to be broken. We stand on a sure foundation with a fixed hope in what the Lord will do for us now and throughout eternity. The enemy may come at you with all forms of deception, but you will not be shaken. The enemy may use someone close to you to bring pain and loss into your life, but the Lord will not allow you to be broken if you are standing on the sure foundation of Jesus Christ. Without this foundation, we would not have a leg to stand on, a hope to hold on to, or a reason to continue. But the Lord is faithful! He will not allow this foundation to be broken. He will not leave you or forsake you! He has promised, and He keeps all His promises. It is on this sure foundation that we place our hopes and establish our faith.

"In the Lord I put my trust; How can you say to my soul, 'Flee as a bird to your mountain'? For look! The wicked bend their bow, They make ready their arrow on the string, That they may shoot secretly at the upright in heart. If the foundations are destroyed, what can the righteous do?" (Psalm 11:1-3)

You can always count on Him! He is your sure foundation. The Lord Jesus is the chief cornerstone, but He is not the only stone the Lord has given to you. He wanted to make certain that you will always be able to stand through all the enemy can throw at you. Therefore, the Lord gave you a foundation made up of many stones. In times of extreme hardship and suffering, you can remember how the foundation of the Temple Solomon was built. The description of this foundation is a powerful reminder of what the Lord has built for you. Solomon put thousands of large and precious stones in the foundation. The Lord has done the same for you. When you remember that He is your foundation also remember that you are now the temple where He lives. You who are the temple of the living God, and you have a foundation made up of many stones.

> *"And the king commanded them to quarry large stones, costly stones, and hewn stones, to lay the foundation of the temple. So Solomon's builders, Hiram's builders, and the Gebalites quarried them; and they prepared timber and stones to build the temple."* (1 Kings 5:17-18)

As I examined the foundations under the Temple Mount in Jerusalem, I was very pleasantly surprised to find that every part of it appeared to be as solid today as when it was first built. It is amazing to see a structure survive for thousands of years with a foundation which remains as strong today as it was in the beginning. That's our God. He did it for the Temple built by Solomon, and He will do it for you. These passages of scripture remind us that we need many strong stones in the foundation for both our lives and our faith. These stones are not all alike. They are not the same size or of the same value, but all are essential. Each one serves a unique and wonderful purpose in God's plan.

INTERCESSOR WARRIORS
NEED A FOUNDATION

You need the entire collection of stones for a sure foundation. Regardless of the physical size of a church, the Lord always provides all the stones necessary to make it strong and permanent.

As I considered the idea of an "entire collection of stones," I thought about how people in the fast food industry learned to manipulate children to increase sales. Several years ago, they introduced the marketing plan of persuading children to collect the cheap plastic toys in the kid's meals. As they used children's TV programs to market their products, they worked to build a desire in the children by encouraging them to collect an entire set of toys. It seemed as if, the children would experience some great loss if they missed even one of these cheap little toys. The children begged and pleaded in order to persuade their parents to take them back to get more. Parents dutifully brought the children to the restaurant every week to collect the set.

But it didn't end there. Next week the first toy in a new set was introduced, and the pressure on the parents continued. The marketing experts had successfully discovered that there is something built into the fabric of our souls which produces a desire for completeness. I believe the Lord put this desire in us for a purpose. And, it was not to help the fast food industry sell more products.

For an entirely different reason, the Lord encourages us to collect the entire set of stones for the foundation of intercessory prayer. When you build a stone arch, every stone is important. If one stone is loose or gets removed, the whole structure may collapse. I watched a group of contractors building a stone arch for the fence around a remodeled home. It was near completion, when one of the workers reached up and touched one of the stone near the capstone. The cement had not had time to set and the little stone fell to the ground. All of the workers immediately scrambled to get away from the arch. As we helplessly watched, the entire structure came tumbling to the ground. After the dust settled, they had to start their work all over again. By itself, that one little stone seemed insignificant, but when it came loose the entire structure collapsed into a heap of disconnected stones.

We wouldn't think of building a house with only part of the foundation. That would obviously be a formula for failure. Yet, people will do things in the spiritual realm which they would never allow to happen in the natural. It is critically important for us to understand that we can't build a spiritual house on a partial foundation. Perhaps you know people who have tried that. An even more foolish mistake is to build with no foundation at all. Remember what Jesus said about this.

> *"But why do you call Me 'Lord, Lord,' and not do the things which I say? Whoever comes to Me, and hears My sayings and does them, I will show you whom he is like: He is like a man building a house, who dug deep and laid the foundation on the rock. And when the flood arose, the stream beat vehemently against that house, and could not shake it, for it was founded on the rock. But he who heard and did nothing is like a man who built a house on the earth without a foundation, against which the stream beat vehemently; and immediately it fell. And the ruin of that house was great."* (Luke 6:46-49)

At the beginning of this year, the Lord said to me over and over, *"It is time to restore the foundations!"* This Word from the Lord turned out to be a call for me to put together all the things He had been releasing to me over a period of three years. In this progressive revelation, the Lord pointed me to these nine stones which make up the foundation for intercessory prayer. He made it clear from the beginning that we need to build with all of the stones and not just the ones we like or more easily understand.

We always struggle with the temptation to focus on the things we like and ignore or forget the things which are difficult or challenging. We simply cannot do this with the foundation of our faith. Ultimately, the Lord Jesus is our sure foundation. As we get into a relationship of obedience with Him, we begin to receive an ever increasing understanding of His plan for our lives. We learn day by day about all the various tools He provides for us to be successful in our mission. We cannot become the kind of intercessor warriors He has anointed us to be without the complete set of foundation stones He has provide

A BRIEF REVIEW

The first stone in the collection we examined in this study was the stone of authority. To succeed in your mission, you must be aware of and use the authority the Lord has given to His intercessors. To be effective in your mission as an intercessor, you must know and understand your God-given authority in prayer. You begin by understanding that God gives authority to all believers. Then, you realize that He has given unique and specific forms of authority to His intercessors. We need to know the extent of that authority in prayer. We must also understand the limitations and stay within our lines of authority. Two scriptures are very important for us to understand in order to function effectively as intercessor warriors.

"The heaven, even the heavens, are the Lord's; but the earth He has given to the children of men." (Psalm 115:16)

"Behold, I give you the authority to trample on serpents and scorpions, and over all the power of the enemy, and nothing shall by any means hurt you." (Luke 10:19)

The second stone the Lord revealed for our foundation was the Word of God. We must take our stand on the Word and remain standing on this rock regardless of what we may have to endure. The Lord releases a word of encouragement to us by showing us how powerful this stone is.

"For the word of God is living and powerful, and sharper than any two-edged sword, piercing even to the division of soul and spirit, and of joints and marrow, and is a discerner of the thoughts and intents of the heart." (Hebrews 4:12)

Your primary offensive weapon for spiritual warfare is the sword of the Spirit. You know that this sword is in reality the Word of God. In order to be effective in this area of your mission, you must possess the sword and strengthen yourself by using it regularly. It needs to be stored in your heart where it will always be available when you need it. The primary lesson to be learned at this point is to always ask yourself if what you are praying is in the Word of God! Is it compatible with the Word? Can you find a specific scriptural reference for what you are praying? If it is not in the Word of God, don't pray for it! Look again at the need you are addressing, find a scripture that will answer that need, and then pray in accordance with the Word of God.

As you consider the third stone in your foundation, there is some really good news in the Word. You are not called to go into battle all alone! Too many people today want to work alone. Many people find it difficult to work cooperatively with others. As a result, they are working with a limited amount of authority and power. This is not the time or place to try to be an army of one. Every soldier knows that we are at our best when we work in teams. People admire groups like the Army Special Forces or Seal Teams. Each member shows great strength, courage, ability, and training. The members of special units like these would never try to do the job alone. Their strength lies in the combined abilities of the entire team.

In addition, trying to work alone is contrary to the specific teachings of the Lord. You cannot expect positive results from disobedient behavior. The Lord will never bless disobedience or any of the works produced by it. Knowing this, you should seek to follow what the Lord taught.

AGREEMENT IS A SPIRITUAL POWER MULTIPLIER

"So Peter was kept in prison, but the church was earnestly praying to God for him. The night before Herod was to bring him to trial, Peter was sleeping between two soldiers, bound with two chains, and sentries stood guard at the entrance. Suddenly an angel of the Lord appeared and a light shone in the cell. He struck Peter on the side and woke him up. "Quick, get up!" he said, and the chains fell off Peter's wrists. Then the angel said to him, "Put on your clothes and sandals." And Peter did so. "Wrap your cloak around you and follow me," the angel told him. Peter followed him out of the prison, but he had no idea that what the angel was doing was really happening; he thought he was seeing a vision. They passed the first and second guards and came to the iron gate leading to the city. It opened for them by itself, and they went through it. When they had walked the length of one street, suddenly the angel left him. Then Peter came to himself and said, "Now I know without a doubt that the Lord sent his angel and rescued me from

Herod's clutches and from everything the Jewish people were anticipating." (Acts 12:5-11, NIV)

This Biblical account is a great illustration of the power of agreement. Peter had been put into prison, and you can be certain that Peter was praying for deliverance with all his heart. But, he was not alone. The entire church was praying for Him. They were not praying little brief prayers occasionally asking, "Lord bless Peter! or Lord help Peter!" This passage tells us that they were earnestly praying. The Message Bible says it this way, *"All the time that Peter was under heavy guard in the jailhouse, the church prayed for him most strenuously."* (Acts 12:5, TMSG) I like that idea of praying strenuously. They were really pressing in with all their spiritual strength seeking an answer from the Lord.

Herod had recently arrested the Apostle James and murdered him. The church didn't want to lose Peter as well. So, they prayed *"strenuously"* and continuously for His release. Notice also that they were praying in agreement. They all wanted the same thing! They were all praying for the same outcome! In doing this, they released the kind of spiritual power that got a mighty response from the Lord. He sent an angel to liberate Peter. When you pray in agreement, you go beyond the simple addition of your influence. In agreement, you actually multiply the power and results. The intercessors in the chruch were obedient to the Lord and received the results He promised:

"Again I say to you that if two of you agree on earth concerning anything that they ask, it will be done for them by My Father in heaven. For where two or three are gathered together in My name, I am there in the midst of them." (Matthew 18:19-20)

Have you ever noticed that great advertisements are not always accurate? The advertisement *"An Army of One"* is a good example. You have probably seen the ad with a single soldier running across the desert with weapons, ammunition, a full pack, and lots of other gear. The message being sent was that one person could take the battle to the enemy and achieve the desired results. But, one soldier alone cannot win the battle, much less the war. The message was not true. However, this ad was very successful for the recruiting stations. It appealed to young people who wanted to become powerful as individuals. It connected with and appealed to a computer gaming generation of people who valued the image of one person defeating an entire army. This ad brought many young people in to the recruiters across the country. But "An Army of One" is a foolish idea to try to implement.

Jesus prayed for the Father to make us one. If Jesus prayed this, it must be important! And we know that He prayed it over and over. When you see something the Lord says or does over and over, be aware that He wants you to know that it is very important. Jesus modeled persistence in prayer, but there is more to the message than simple persistence. The Lord wants you to know that the kingdom of God is about unity; that unity produces agreement; and agreement releases spiritual power.

"Now I am no longer in the world, but these are in the world, and I come to You. Holy Father, keep through Your name those whom You have given Me, that they may be one as We are." (John 17:11)

I recommend a study of John chapter 17 for every believer, but especially for all intercessor warriors. One of the great lessons in this chapter is the powerful focus Jesus put on unity. We need be one in spirit and in one accord when we pray. Paul taught this truth when he wrote:

"There is one body and one Spirit, just as you were called in one hope of your calling; one Lord, one faith,

one baptism; one God and Father of all, who is above all, and through all, and in you all." (Ephesians 4:4-6)

In so many parts of the body of Christ, people are sowing strive and discord more than harmony and unity. I believe this is one of the main reasons people fail to see the desired results from their prayers. Two people in the same prayer meeting may be praying for opposite results, canceling out both requests. Part of the group may be praying to move in one direction, while the remainder are praying to go a different way. How can the Lord answer these opposing prayers? It is important for a group praying together to get agreement before the time of prayer begins. To be effective, intercessor warriors must be committed to preventing disharmony and disunity. If someone in the group is sowing discord among the members, it must be dealt with before continuing with the prayer time. Proverbs 6:16-19 lists seven things God hates.

"These six things the Lord hates, Yes, seven are an abomination to Him: A proud look, A lying tongue, Hands that shed innocent blood, A heart that devises wicked plans, Feet that are swift in running to evil, A false witness who speaks lies, And one who sows discord among brethren."

Please take note of the final thing on the list: "*. . . one who sows discord among brethren.*" (verse 6:19b) Strife and divisions result in a powerless prayer life. The Lord goes beyond merely disliking this. The writer reminds us that the Lord hates these behaviors. They are an abomination to Him. But, how many people really realize how God feels. My experience has been that the people who are causing strife feel justified in what they are doing. They have taken up some cause to correct all of God's other servants. Some even claim it is the work of the Lord.

This is not just an Old Testament word for us. Take another look at the teachings of Jesus, and you will quickly see that we are not to judge and condemn other people; especially those in the household of faith. Paul teaches the same thing in many of his letters to various churches. Yet, we have not seen much focus on these teachings in recent times. Consider what Paul wrote to the church in Corinth:

"I fed you with milk and not with solid food; for until now you were not able to receive it, and even now you are still not able; for you are still carnal. For where there are envy, strife, and divisions among you, are you not carnal and behaving like mere men?" (1 Corinthians 3:2-3)

When we have envy, strife, and divisions in the church it points to a spiritual condition of carnality which needs immediate resolution. If the church is carnally minded, it is hazardous to our witness to the world. If the intercessory prayer team is carnally minded, it is a tragedy for the kingdom of God. God will not bless it! We must first deal with the issues between sisters and brothers before coming to the throne of God with our request.

On the other hand, when we work together, God multiplies power. Several scriptures point to the multiplication of power which comes with unity. One of my favorites is located in the book of Leviticus.

"Five of you shall chase a hundred, and a hundred of you shall put ten thousand to flight; your enemies shall fall by the sword before you." "Leviticus 26:8"

Have you ever done the math on this promise? If five can chase a hundred enemy soldiers, then each one is chasing twenty. However, if you raise the size of your group up to one hundred working in unity, then each one is enabled to chase one hundred of the enemy. This higher level of unity has given a five-fold increase in the effectiveness of each person in the group. You can clearly see that this promise is about multiplication and not simple addition. You don't merely add to each other's effectiveness in prayer. Together, you multiply both the power and the results of your work.

Let's take this idea of agreement one step further. Consider what happens when you add God to your group. When you get into unity and agreement with God, you have access to His power. This is one of the powerful lessons Jesus was trying to teach in John, chapter 17.

Now, let's take it another step further. The power of agreement can be spread out over time. Time and distance do not limit the work of the Holy Spirit. The Lord begins to teach the disciples that this unity extends to all believers throughout all time. In the Lord and through the work of the Holy Spirit, we become one with all believers throughout history. When we stand in agreement with them, we continue to multiply the power and effectiveness of our prayers. When we pray the prayers they prayed, we are increasing the number we are using to multiply the results. I believe this is part of the power of the *"great cloud of witnesses"* referenced in Hebrews 12:1. As you study the teachings of Jesus, notice how often He makes reference to multiplication effect coming through agreement.

> *"I do not pray for these alone, but also for those who will believe in Me through their word; that they all may be one, as You, Father, are in Me, and I in You; that they also may be one in Us, that the world may believe that You sent Me."* (John 17:20-21)

When we pray in accordance with the Word of God and in agreement with Him and other believers, God adds His power to the authority He has already given to us. I like to illustrate this idea by using some terms related to mechanical power. With God you are praying in turbo mode! Your prayers become super charged as His power is added to your authority. Remember: when you mix His super with your natural, the result is something supernatural. I like supernatural results from my prayers. How about you?

An additional benefit to the kingdom of God is that this unity in love is our witness to the world. This often produces better results than our sermons, arguments, and human wisdom. Consider what it might do for our outreach, if we could truly be united and treat each other with the love of Father God and Christ Jesus. The world would then know that the message is true. It would break through all the enemy's power of deception and reveal the truth of God's love.

"I in them, and You in Me; that they may be made perfect in one, and that the world may know that You have sent Me, and have loved them as You have loved Me." (John 17:23)

Nothing looks worse to the world than Christians quarrelling, backbiting, criticizing, and blaming one another. It seems as if many Christians spend more time attacking each other than they spend attacking the enemy. Pause and reflect on this. Remember who the enemy is:

"For we do not wrestle against flesh and blood, but against principalities, against powers, against the rulers of the darkness of this age, against spiritual hosts of wickedness in the heavenly places." (Ephesians 6:12)

JESUS ALWAYS PUT PEOPLE INTO TEAMS

"And He called the twelve to Himself, and began to send them out two by two, and gave them power over unclean spirits." (Mark 6:7)

Looking at this passage of scripture, I was reminded again that we have too many people trying to do the job alone. When Jesus sent people out, the minimum number was always two. This minimum number consisted of people He had personally trained for some time. These were people who were with Him night and day, seven days a week over a period of two or more years. Even with that time in His presence and all the personal training, they still needed each other to accomplish the mission. Teamwork seems to have been a set pattern in Jesus' ministry.

"After this the Lord appointed seventy–two others and sent them two by two ahead of him to every town and place where he was about to go." (Luke 10:1, NIV)

During my military career, I heard people being labeled as "the Lone Ranger." This name always pointed to someone who was unable or unwilling to work with others and always tried to accomplish every task alone. People with this label were often seen trying to gain special recognition for themselves without regard to the needs of others. Instead of being characterized as a person who was brave, gifted, or wise they were more often seen as foolish risk takers. Being referred to as a "Lone Ranger" was not a good label for anyone who wanted a career in the military. Teamwork is essential to success.

The Lone Ranger was a fictional character first introduced in the early days of radio. No one seems certain about who originated the idea, but it caught on and this fictional character became very popular on both radio and television. According to the story, he had been a Texas Ranger who moved further west to fight for helpless people in order to right all the wrongs on the western frontier. The name of the character indicated that he was alone, but this was never the case. The Lone Ranger had a faithful Native American companion named Tonto. As a child, I watched the program and even at a very early age, I began to wonder where the Lone Ranger would be without Tonto? Even in the natural, we know that teamwork is essential to success. Solomon certainly had this in mind when he wrote:

"Two are better than one, because they have a good reward for their labor. For if they fall, one will lift up his companion. But woe to him who is alone when he falls, for he has no one to help him up." (Ecclesiastes 4:9-10)

According to Solomon, as a general rule, two are better than one. They are able to produce more and the shared reward is greater than for one acting alone. If one is down, the other can lift them back up. A ministry of encouragement should emerge from every team of two or more. By taking turns building one another up, both can remain strong and effective. Conversely, those who work alone have no one to help them when they fall down or face failure. Woe is a powerful concept. It is like a curse. It is difficult to shake it off and it tends to push people toward failure.

On a military team, it is important to have someone to cover your back. The back always refers to a blind spot in our visual field. Enemies try to find and attack these points of vulnerability. If you have a companion, that person can watch your back. Soldiers have learned to fight back to back for maximum effectiveness. Who has your back? Of course the other question is whose back are you covering with protection? The very nature of intercession should indicate that it is a matter of extending protective prayers over someone else.

If people operating strictly in the natural have learned and implemented this strategy for maximum results, shouldn't believers do the same? If it works in the physical realm, how much more powerful is it in the spiritual? Solomon gives an easily verifiable illustration. Many instructors ask students to try this formula and see for themselves. Try it yourself and you will see the multiplication of power in a cord of three strands.

> *"Though one may be overpowered by another, two can withstand him. And a threefold cord is not quickly broken."* (Ecclesiastes 4:12, NKJV [*A cord of three strands is not quickly broken."* NIV])

Most believers tend to think Jesus could do anything He wanted to do at any time He chose to do it. But that is not what the Bible teaches. Consider carefully the words of Jesus in John 5:30a (NIV), *"By myself I can do nothing;"* For many believers that is difficult to grasp. After all, wasn't He God? Yes! He was and is one of the members of the Trinity. However, Jesus gave up the riches of Heaven to come down to earth and work out our salvation. In order to accomplish this huge undertaking, Jesus needed the power of the Lord to assist Him with the work. We must always remember that the Lord not only taught truthful principles, He also modeled them. As He told us to work in agreement, He demonstrated it by always working in agreement with the Father and the Holy Spirit.

> *"One day as he was teaching, Pharisees and teachers of the law, who had come from every village of Galilee and from Judea and Jerusalem, were sitting there. And the power of the Lord was present for him to heal the sick."* (Luke 5:17, NIV)

As I looked more deeply into this passage of scripture a challenging thought came into my mind. If special mention was made that *"the power of the Lord was present for him to heal the sick"* on that day, were there days when the power was not available. This led me to another passage of scripture.

"Jesus said to them, 'Only in his hometown, among his relatives and in his own house is a prophet without honor.' He could not do any miracles there, except lay his hands on a few sick people and heal them. And he was amazed at their lack of faith." (Mark 6:4-6, NIV)

Most people can accept theologically that it was Jesus' unity with the Father and the indwelling Holy Spirit that gave Him the spiritual power to heal and work miracles. But this passage from Mark indicates that He also needed the agreement of the people's faith in order to work miracles and heal all of the sick. This is a much tougher idea to accept. Did Jesus need to be in agreement with other people in order to experience the fullness of power to do miracles? What do you think? Now consider this, if it was necessary for Jesus to be in agreement with other people, what about you and me?

This is an area of our theological understanding in which it is especially important for us to have clarity. If we understand both what Jesus was teaching and modeling in this part of the Bible, it will help us to understand His promise that we will be able to do what He did and even more. Like Jesus, we can only do these things through the power of God and the work of the Holy Spirit in us. Remember that Jesus not only taught us what we could and should do for the Father. He also modeled it. If Jesus could do everything by Himself, we could not possibly imitate Him. We could not possibly become like Him. We could never expect to fulfill the ministry the Lord has anointed us to do. Like Jesus, we need others to stand in agreement with us to release the power of God into the work of ministry. Perhaps Jesus was more like us than we have previously understood.

Now, consider that there is an even higher level of agreement than two or three of us working together. Imagine being on a team with Jesus as one of the members. That is exactly what the Bible teaches. If we love Him and obey Him, He and the Father come to live in us. In addition, the Holy Spirit is given to live in us forever. Wow! What a team! Think about it: two or more of us plus Jesus Christ, Father God, and the Holy Spirit – now that is a powerful team!

Now think again about those prayers in the Bible I encouraged you to pray over yourself and others. Considering what we have just gone through in our faith walk with this study, pray this prayer over yourself again and receive the full impact of all that it means. Later, pray it with this understanding over the members of your intercessory team. Think about what you will release when you pray this in faith and agreement.

"For this reason I bow my knees to the Father of our Lord Jesus Christ, from whom the whole family in heaven and earth is named, that He would grant you, according to the riches of His glory, to be strengthened with might through His Spirit in the inner man, that Christ may dwell in your hearts through faith; that you, being rooted and grounded in love, may be able to comprehend with all the saints what is the width and length and depth and height—to know the love of Christ which passes knowledge; that you may be filled with all the fullness of God." (Ephesians 3:14-19)

Look again at this teaching of Jesus when He said that His followers would do more than He did. For many believers that is difficult to fully grasp. If you are still struggling with this idea, consider Paul's teaching to the Ephesian Church. Now let the Word of God pray this prayer over you! Read it as if Paul was present and praying this for you right now. Hear in the depth of your spirit these words: *"that you may be filled with all the fullness of God."* Wow! Can you imagine that? Well, you had better be able to do more than imagine it if you want to succeed in your mission. You need to receive it, thank God for it, do all these things, and then give God all the glory in the name of Jesus! Amen!

If you are still struggling, go back to those prayers of Jesus in John, chapters 14-17. Pray them out loud and hear the voice of Jesus speaking to your spirit and making it real in your life and ministry. Do it right now with the prayer below:

> *"Most assuredly, I say to you, he who believes in Me, the works that I do he will do also; and greater works than these he will do, because I go to My Father. And whatever you ask in My name, that I will do, that the Father may be glorified in the Son. If you ask anything in My name, I will do it."* (John 14:12-14)

Where do you see these *"greater works"* happening today? Are you seeing them in your own life and ministry? If not, what do you need to do to raise the bar in your own walk of faith? Since Jesus spoke and confirmed these things, they have become foundation stones for us. If you are not experiencing this, you need to get back on the foundation and pray in unity. We need to raise both the level of our faith and the level of our expectations.

WORKING IN AGREEMENT
IS A MULTIPLIER

> *"Again I say to you that if two of you agree on earth concerning anything that they ask, it will be done for them by My Father in heaven. For where two or three are gathered together in My name, I am there in the midst of them."* (Matthew 18:19-20)

This is often referred to as the spiritual law of agreement. When Jesus gave this promise it became an absolute. Begin to see more and more that this statement is an absolute. It is a spiritual law based on the teaching and promises of Jesus. Think about how much of our power we have given up by not standing in agreement. Many people lack assurance when they are praying alone. If relatively new believers can get on a prayer team and find out that others are praying the same things they are seeking and are getting Jesus' kind of results, it can really build their faith, courage, and self-confidence. I want more multiplication! How about you?

As we learned in the previous lesson, praying in agreement with the Word is a ministry multiplier. It helps to keep us working within the will of God, and it adds God's power to achieve His results. The Word of God becomes a witness along with our spirit that what we are praying is right. Remember, God never leads us away from His Word. God never contradicts His Word! It is absolute! Now we have added another layer of the spiritual power of agreement. We are in agreement with the Lord and with the Word of God.

Linking up with other believers and establishing agreement with them is God's will for us. Even if you don't understand it, do it in faith and obedience. When you stand outside the will of God, you only have human power. You cannot accomplish much in the spiritual realm if you are limited to human authority and power. Always remember that an army of one can be taken down by one enemy shot.

Another aspect of agreement is that it helps to foster and insure both personal and team spiritual accountability. The validity of our witness and our testimony are both enhanced when we stand in agreement. This is one of the oldest principles in the Bible and Paul re-introduced it to the church in Corinth.

"By the mouth of two or three witnesses every word shall be established." (2 Corinthians 13:1b)

Agreement also places a powerful limitation on the enemy. The primary tactic the enemy uses is to confuse us with man-made rules and doctrines. By continuing to push these on us, the enemy begins to build a veil of deception over the eyes of the church as well as over individual believers. At its worst this deception can evolve into a form of delusion. A deluded church is a powerless church. A deluded individual is a powerless individual. But, consider this: It is difficult for two people to share a delusion. As we cover each other's backs, we can clarify the areas of deception and reveal any delusions which the enemy may try to bring upon us.

As we labor together to establish and maintain agreement, we help each other stay accountable to the Word. God gave us the law of agreement to bond us together and strengthen us for every good work.

GOD IS THE GREATEST POWER MULTIPLIER

"One man of you shall chase a thousand, for the Lord your God is He who fights for you, as He promised you." (Joshua 23:10)

This word from the Lord takes the effectiveness of agreement up another level. In the scriptures we examined earlier, believers were elevated in stages. First, they went to the level of chasing twenty each. As more stood in agreement, they were enabled to chase one hundred each. Now, with God's help, each one can chase a thousand. Getting into agreement with God increases your effectiveness quickly and exponentially. This must be why Jesus prayed for this unity over and over. If it was important enough for Jesus to persistently pray for it, it should be that important to us as well.

Ultimately, all power and authority belong to God. However, it is unbiblical to take the position that it is only found there. Over and over we read about the Lord making it clear that He delegates authority. This is one of the most powerful spiritual principles in the gospel of the kingdom of God. He has all authority and He is the delegator of authority. He expects us to operate in the kingdom with all the authority He has given. When we do that in accordance with His Word and His will, He adds His power with our authority to accomplish His goals and objectives. As you examine this authority, you will clearly see that we are commissioned and anointed by the Lord to use His delegated authority in our intercessory prayers.

When ordering supplies and equipment in the military, I was never certain about what I would actually receive until I learned to use sole source justifications. When it comes to things of the kingdom, it is wise to work the same way. Remember that God is your sole (soul) source for provisions, strength, power, and authority.

"Before I learned to answer you, I wandered all over the place, but now I'm in step with your Word. You are good, and the source of good; train me in your goodness." (Psalm 119:67-68, TMSG))

One powerful principle the Bible identifies for the kingdom of God is that power is available to those who have received His delegated authority. If everyone in the kingdom knew this and operated in the manner prescribed in the Word, there would be no stopping the moves of God in the world. But, tragically, many in the church seem to believe in a powerless Christian life. Many believers have embraced this false teachings as a doctrine of the church. However, I am convinced that God wants to raise up another generation of true disciples who will accept what He has given and will move forth to accomplish His purpose. He is looking for a generation who will accept authority, stand in agreement, and become fully equipped intercessor warriors.

It's God's will that we have power for His purpose. There is no arrogance or audacity in the use of God's power. The moment you think it comes from you, it's gone. The proper use of God's power is with humble submission.

I urge you to let God train you to be a powerful prayer warrior. If you don't think you know how to do it, ask God. The Holy Spirit was given for this specific purpose. He will guide you into all truth, and then embolden and empower you for every good work.

God answers prayers like this. David discovered that in His prayer life. God's answer is given to David in Psalm 91

"Because he has set his love upon Me, therefore I will deliver him; I will set him on high, because he has known My name. He shall call upon Me, and I will answer him; I will be with him in trouble; I will deliver him and honor him. With long life I will satisfy him, and show him My salvation." (Psalm 91:14-16)

Isn't this what you have hoped for and longed for?

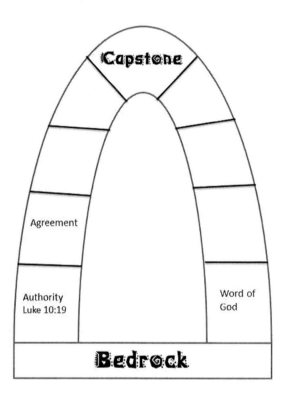

Agreement – The Third Stone in the Foundation

CHAPTER 4

THE STONE OF GOD'S WILL

ЖЖ

"Epaphras, who is one of you, a bondservant of Christ, greets you, always laboring fervently for you in prayers, that you may stand perfect and complete in all the will of God. For I bear him witness that he has a great zeal for you, and those who are in Laodicea, and those in Hierapolis." (Colossians 4:12-13)

There are some passages in the Bible which I have read over and over before suddenly seeing a glaring truth. Each time I read them in the past, I had somehow overlooked a very significant part of the message. Has that ever happened to you? I mentioned earlier in the book how much I admire Epaphras as an intercessor warrior. I read about him over and over during my scheduled times of reading through the entire Bible, and thought I knew all I needed to know. However, as I prepared to teach this lesson I went back again to the passage above and read it over and over. The thing which first caught my eye was the idea that Epaphras was *"laboring fervently"* for people in his prayers. I liked that idea and prayed that someone would pray for me in the same way. Next, I noticed that Paul said Epaphras had great zeal for the Colossians. I liked that too.

I would love to have people praying for me with great zeal. To me this was a good lesson and I was pleased.

However, the Lord had something else in mind for me. Somewhere, embedded in this passage, was a nugget of truth or a pearl of great price, but I hadn't seen it yet. It took me a long time to catch it. Suddenly, I experienced something like a blinding light revelation. Perhaps you have already seen it. Paul's words spoke to me in the depth of my spirit. Epaphras ultimately prayed for the Colossian Church to be perfect and complete in "***all the will of God.***" Epaphras wanted the people he loved to fully walk in and live up to the perfect will of God.

Wow! I wondered how often I had prayed that way over someone else. At that moment, I couldn't remember even one time when I had actually prayed for another person to be "*perfect and complete in all the will of God.*" However, since this revelation came, I can no longer count how many times I have prayed this for others. Read it again and soak it in! It seems so simple, but it is so profound. I pray that you "may stand perfect and complete in all the will of God." There I did it again.

As I mentioned earlier, we don't know very much about Epaphras. What we do know is that Paul saw him as a prayer warrior. I don't think that Paul was very easily impressed. Yet, this man's prayers touched Paul in some very special ways, and hundreds of years later his story is touching me right now. This is the impact of a man who prayers fervently for others seeking the will of God in their lives. It sounds simple when you hear it, but it is a challenge to implement in your own prayer life or in your intercessory group. Epaphras was a man who impressed Paul with his zeal for people as he made intercession for them. I wondered about you and me. Are we impressing others with our zeal for prayer? Is anyone taking note of the amazing way we pray for others? Wouldn't you like to have an intercessor like Epaphras? Wouldn't you like to be a prayer warrior like Epaphras? What steps would you need to take right now to become more like him in your prayer life?

Sometimes when we read through a book, we just move through it without stopping to process the content in our own lives. I encourage you to slow down for a few moments and think this through. Seriously consider the question: What kind of intercessor warrior do you want to become? What do you need to do to move to a higher level? What do you need to ask in prayer to release a higher anointing on your prayers than you are currently experiencing? Remember, Jesus said, "Ask, and it will be given to you; seek, and you will find; knock, and it will be opened to you. For everyone who asks receives, and he who seeks finds, and to him who knocks it will be opened." (Matthew 7:7-8)

DO YOU WANT TO BECOME A PRAYER WARRIOR?

"Likewise the Spirit also helps in our weaknesses. For we do not know what we should pray for as we ought, but the Spirit Himself makes intercession for us with groanings which cannot be uttered. Now He who searches the hearts knows what the mind of the Spirit is, because He makes intercession for the saints according to the will of God." (Romans 8:26-27)

After receiving revelation knowledge about Epaphras and his prayers of intercession, I went back to the passage above. Did you notice that the Holy Spirit prays in a way which is similar to Epaphras? Now I know where Epaphras received his gift for intercession. He was obediently following the leadership of the Holy Spirit. When the Holy Spirit prays for you, He does so "***according to the will of God***." The Holy Spirit prays for us with "**groanings**" which we cannot utter. To me, that sounds like Epaphras fervently laboring in his prayers for others. Like the groans of travail uttered by a woman as she delivers a baby, the Holy Spirit fervently labors for you to be born anew and live as a new creation in Jesus Christ!

Do you want to become an intercessor like Epaphras? Do you want to pray for people the same way the Holy Spirit intercedes for you? Do you want to become an intercessor warrior? If you do, you need to build on a solid foundation. Do you want others to pray for you as Epaphras prayed? Do you want them to pray for you like the Holy Spirit prays for you? Then you need to help them build and stand on the solid foundation which the Lord has established for us!

Warriors who are called and anointed by the Lord as intercessors must strive to always be found standing on the firm foundation given by God. They understand their role and responsibilities. Like Epaphras, these valiant prayer warriors are totally dedicated to their task.

A BRIEF REVIEW

Intercessors begin by standing on the stone of authority. They begin by giving serious study to the Word of God in order to fully understand their spiritual authority in prayer. They make a commitment to be obedient to the leadership of the Holy Spirit, and seek His guidance to continue to grow in their understanding of kingdom authority. Their goal is to pray with the kind of authority that will release the power of God into the situation. To be effective, they need to know the boundaries established by the Lord. The "Good News" is that the boundaries are greater than most think in the beginning.

Next, intercessor warriors learn to pray in accordance with God's Word. They also learn to pray God's Word as it is written in the Bible. Intercessors also learn to pray the prayers which are given as examples in the Word. God always acts in accordance with His Word. Praying His word releases great power. You are truly wasting your time if you are praying against the

Word of God. The "Good News" is that if your prayers are founded in the Word, they will work.

Then, these intercessor warriors have come to the understanding that God's plan is for teams to be praying in agreement. Believers praying in the power of agreement are one of the most powerful forces on earth. Unfortunately, we don't see much of this kind of prayer in the church. Division, un-forgiveness, strife, and discord work to cancel most of the prayers of those who have not learned to work in teams in order to strengthen and build each other up.

"As iron sharpens iron, so one man sharpens another." (Proverbs 27:17, NIV)

In this lesson, we're looking at the fourth stone in the foundation. The fourth stone is the "will of God." Note: Epaphras prayed for God's will to be done in Colossae. He knew God wanted them to be perfect and complete. I believe that Paul was one of those who stood in agreement with Epaphras. This is part of the reason why Paul used him as an example for others.

PRAY WHAT GOD WANTS TO HAPPEN

This is very different from ending every prayer with the disclaimer, "if it be your will?" This is most often used by people who have no idea what God's will is for themselves or anyone else. This is the prayer of a double minded person. It is a very ineffective way of praying, because there is no faith in a prayer which ends this way. The prayers of double minded people do not get answered. More precisely, double minded people should expect nothing when they pray. People usually add this phrase (if it be your will?) after praying in their own will instead of God's will. By saying, "if it be your will?" these people are actually admitting that they do not know or understand God's will. They are admitting that they don't know

God's will for themselves or for those being mentioned in their intercessory prayers. When you pray this way, you are actually cancelling out whatever it is that you are asking in prayer. To pray effectively, you need to access the wisdom of Father God. But how do you access His wisdom? It is actually very simple and easy. All you have to do is ask Father God who is your source of supply for every spiritual blessing in Christ Jesus.

"If any of you lacks wisdom, he should ask God, who gives generously to all without finding fault, and it will be given to him. But when he asks, he must believe and not doubt, because he who doubts is like a wave of the sea, blown and tossed by the wind. That man should not think he will receive anything from the Lord; he is a double–minded man, unstable in all he does." (James 1:5-8, NIV)

When a prayer ends with the disclaimer, "if it be your will," I believe it is a double-minded prayer. It seems to me that this type of prayer emerged from people with a twisted under-standing of Jesus' prayer in the garden.

"Again, a second time, He went away and prayed, saying, "O My Father, if this cup cannot pass away from Me unless I drink it, Your will be done." (Matthew 26:42)

Jesus' prayer was a prayer of obedience. He knew what the will of God was and He submitted to it. He acknowledged that He would like to be spared the suffering of the cross, but also confessed that He would willingly submit to and obey the will of the Father. Jesus' prayer was a prayer of faith, obedience, and single-mindedness.

We will look at another scripture which is helpful in devel-oping an understanding of the kind of prayers which are based on the will of God. Like Jesus, Paul had received a revelation and understood the way in which he would suffer and die. He had no intention of turning back from his commitment to proclaim the gospel of the Kingdom. In fact, Paul was ready to die for his Lord. However, his fellow workers didn't want him to be taken from them. They had been weeping and begging for a different outcome. When they realized that they were not persuading Paul, they changed the way in which they were praying. Read the scripture below aloud and meditate on it to draw out all the wisdom you can receive from it.

> *"Then Paul answered, 'What do you mean by weeping and breaking my heart? For I am ready not only to be bound, but also to die at Jerusalem for the name of the Lord Jesus.' So when he would not be persuaded, we ceased, saying, 'The will of the Lord be done.'"* (Acts 21:13-14)

You will notice that in verse 14 Paul's companions changed the way they were praying and started to pray for the will of God to be done. They were not necessarily happy with it, but they knew better than to pray against the will of God. Begin to examine your own prayers. Are they based on faith or do you add phrases to take the pressure off in case things don't change? If you see some double-minded prayers in your own experience begin to purge them out of your vocabulary and ask the Holy Spirit to give you the wisdom to do it effectively.

You may ask: "If it's His will, why doesn't He just do it? At this point in your study, how would you answer that question? The answer is found in the first foundation stone. Remember that God has given you authority over your area of ministry and service. He's waiting for you to call on His power and authority. He is waiting for you to activate His will in your life. Here is an important point to remember: If it is His will already, you are simply activating it through your prayers.

HOW DO YOU PRAY THE WILL OF GOD?

It is not really that difficult in most cases to pray the will of God. In the section below, I will give you several examples of praying for the will of God to be done in someone's life. You can also pray this way for yourself. In each case, begin with locating a passage in the Bible which identifies something which is God's will for you or those for whom you are praying.

"This is the will of the Father who sent Me, that of all He has given Me I should lose nothing, but should raise it up at the last day. And this is the will of Him who sent Me, that everyone who sees the Son and believes in Him may have everlasting life; and I will raise him up at the last day." (John 6:39-40)

In this passage, Jesus identifies several things which are God's will. First, He made it clear that it is not God's will for any of those given to Him by the Father to be lost. Turning that from a negative to a positive statement, we see that it is God's will for all those who come to Jesus to be with Him forever. Next, He says clearly that it is God's will for everyone who sees and believes in Jesus to have everlasting life. Finally, Jesus says that it is God's will for believers to be raised from the dead at the last day. As we pray for others, we can stand on the foundation stone of God's will, and ask for all these things in complete assurance. We know that He wants people to see Jesus, come to Jesus, believe in Jesus, belong to Jesus, have eternal life, and be raised from the dead. As you pray these things over others, you add to your prayers the prayers of Jesus and the will of God. Wow! That is real authority and power in prayer. Paul also taught this concept to his spiritual son, Timothy:

"For this is good and acceptable in the sight of God our Savior, who desires all men to be saved and to come to the knowledge of the truth. For there is one God and one Mediator between God and men, the Man Christ Jesus." (1 Timothy 2:3-5)

We can pray all three of these things for others with full confidence that they are in the Word of God and that they are in the known will of God. They are in the written Word of God, the living Word of God (Jesus the Christ), and the teachings of the apostles. When you pray for these things, pray with authority knowing it is God's will. There is no need for begging and pleading. These are prayers to authoritatively decree and release the awesome power of God to cause these spiritual realities to manifest.

Take a moment or two to work through another example. When you intercede for your children and grandchildren, is it God's will that they be saved, protected, and blessed? Examine the passages below and see it for yourself. When you examine the scriptures, read them out loud, and receive the promises as your own. When you do this, you activate your faith and release God's power to bring about the promised results.

"Even so it is not the will of your Father who is in heaven that one of these little ones should perish." (Matthew 18:14)

"The Lord has been mindful of us; He will bless us; He will bless the house of Israel; He will bless the house of Aaron. He will bless those who fear the Lord, both small and great. May the Lord give you increase more and more, you and your children. May you be blessed by the Lord, Who made heaven and earth." (Psalm 115:12-15)

Our loving and faithful, Father God doesn't want a single one of these little children hurt or lost. He wants them to be blessed. He wants them to have *"increase, more and more."* When you pray for them, do it with real spiritual authority based on the Word of God. You don't have to beg and plead for God to do the things which He has already promised. You don't have to cry out in uncertainty about the things He has already stated are His desired outcomes.

Now, you can intercede with the full authority God has given you over your family members, with the authority of the Word of God, and in accordance with the known will of God. The words you speak and the tone of your voice should reflect the authority the Father has given to you. Let all your intercessory prayers be spoken with authority and power. Let the devil hear it in your voice and see the fruit of faith in your demeanor. Remember that you are activating God's will as you pray with the authority He has given you.

"Ask, and it will be given to you; seek, and you will find; knock, and it will be opened to you. For everyone who asks receives, and he who seeks finds, and to him who knocks it will be opened." (Matthew 7:7-8)

Many of the good gifts and perfect gifts of God are missed because people just don't ask. Remember what James, the brother of Jesus, said in James 4:2b: *"Yet you do not have because you do not ask."* It always amazes me to see people who call themselves Christians becoming energized to fight against the choice of others to believe the teachings of Jesus. They quickly raise all kinds of arguments against these spiritual laws and give examples of their unanswered prayers. In saying these things, they are confessing their own double-mindedness People who ar double minded should expect nothing when they pray without faith.

The next time you see this happen in a fellow church member, analyze it based on the teaching above about praying the Word of God and the Will of God using the authority given by Jesus. Do their prayers really measure up to the standard which activates the power of God? Usually, they are far from actually praying this way. James pointed this out immediately after the example above. He said that sometimes people are asking for the wrong things. *"You ask and do not receive, because you ask amiss, that you may spend it on your pleasures."* (James 4:3)

This is exactly why it's so important to pray the will of God. It insures that you are asking with the right motives, and it releases the power of God for things to manifest. It is God's will for us to accept His calling to be intercessor warriors. We are the disciples of Jesus and He is our number one intercessor. The Holy Spirit intercedes for us. Paul urges all believers to pick up the challenge and pray without ceasing.

> *"I urge, then, first of all, that requests, prayers, intercession and thanksgiving be made for everyone—for kings and all those in authority, that we may live peaceful and quiet lives in all godliness and holiness."* (1 Timothy 2:1-2, NIV)

HOW CAN WE KNOW GOD'S WILL?

After serving more than 44 years as a pastor, I have identified one question I have been asked most often by immature believers. Some of these people I refer to as immature have been church members for a long time, but have not progressed in their faith or understanding. They have not moved forward with their discipleship training. Paul describes people like this as the ones who still need milk although they should be eating solid food by now. When they ask about knowing the will of God, they are not sincerely seeking that knowledge. You can pick this up right away when they ask with a hostile and challenging tone of voice, "How can I possibly come to know the will of God?" This is usually followed by a barrage of reasons why it is unknown and all of their excuses are attempts to place the blame on God for their problem and failures.

Please forgive me, but this kind of questioning along with all the blaming of God always makes my blood boil. I don't want to be unkind, but this question really bothers me. I wrestled with this for a long time to find out why it grates on me so much. Bear with me as I attempt to explain my reaction.

When people ask this, they usually have their guns loaded to fight against anything you may say. They are not really open to learn anything new about Jesus or Father God. They want to point blame rather than being open to a new revelation or understanding. I quickly learned that many people who ask this are not really seeking information, and it is useless to attempt to provide an answer. Some are trying to justify the things they want to happen in their lives which are totally focused on the desires of the flesh. Others try to justify seeking all the material resources which will make them comfortable and happy while neglecting the needs of others. As James says, they are asking amiss. You can know with certainty that they are not open to hear what you have to say.

When they ask about the will of God, it is little more than a veiled accusation against our loving Father God whose glory is His goodness. Their arguments are based on a belief that He cannot be trusted to provide what they desire. When I hear people talking like this I wonder what kind of image they have of God? Do they think He is some kind of miser who withholds because He doesn't want to let go of the things He possesses? Do they think that He is not a good Father? Listen to what Jesus said about the generosity of the Father:

> *"If you then, being evil, know how to give good gifts*
> *to your children, how much more will your Father who*

is in heaven give good things to those who ask Him!"
(Matthew 7:11)

Notice first that Jesus makes it clear that it is not Father God who is evil. He is a better parent than anyone on Earth and He is more generous than all of us combined. It may be uncomfortable, but we need to check on our own spiritual condition from time to time. Ask yourself a few questions. Have you ever wondered about why God hasn't revealed His will more clearly to you? Have you sometimes felt like He is purposely withholding blessings from you? Do you sometimes suspect that He's giving you bad things to teach you a lesson? The enemy would like to plant these kinds of thoughts in all of us. In fact that is exactly what he did to the children of Israel through Baal worship. The demons behind the idols tried to tell people that they were better providers than God. When the children of Israel fell for this talk and went into idolatry, they quickly found out who their provider had been and how bad it was to lose that provision.

Listen carefully to what Jesus is teaching. He says that the Father wants to give us good things when we ask. It is okay to ask! It is God's will to bless you and give you the resources you need to live well and to serve Him. It is His will for you to prosper, be in good health, and have more than enough so you can share with others. James pointed this out so clearly in one of my favorite passages in the Bible:

"Do not be deceived, my beloved brethren. Every good gift and every perfect gift is from above, and comes down from the Father of lights, with whom there is no variation or shadow of turning. Of His own will He brought us forth by the word of truth, that we might be a kind of firstfruits of His creatures." (James 1:16-18)

James begins by telling you not to be deceived. There is so much deception in the world today. There are evil spirits in our midst who want to deceive us. The devil has been trying throughout human history to convince God's people that their Father in Heaven is withholding the best things from them. This was the ploy he used with Adam and Eve in the garden. It is the same strategy he has used in all the centuries since the garden, and he will certainly try to use it on you until you resolve the issue once and for all. Jesus says, "Even an evil parent doesn't treat a child like this." So, how can we accuse our wonderful Father God of such terrible behavior?

Imagine an adult child getting on some television talk show and saying, "I just never knew what my parents wanted. I really wanted to please them. I tried very hard, but I just couldn't get it out of them. It was like they were keeping some big secret, and I could only please them if I guessed what it was and then did it." What would you think of a parent who actually did that? Isn't that what many people are saying about God. They are saying, "It's your fault God because you didn't tell me what you wanted. Why didn't you make your will known to me? Why did you hide it from me?"

How could any born again, Bible believing disciple of Jesus Christ actually believe that Father God hides His will? How can they see our loving God as being that cruel? Listen to what He Himself has been saying for thousands of years:

> "*'For I know the plans I have for you,' declares the Lord, 'plans to prosper you and not to harm you, plans to give you hope and a future.'*" (Jeremiah 29:11, NIV)

The amazing and wonderful love of the Father should compel you to know and to live in His will. When you are able to do this, it will show in your prayer life. It is God's will that you have every perfect gift. Read the message of James again. Read it out loud and let it sink into your heart.

"Every good gift and every perfect gift is from above, and comes down from the Father of lights, with whom there is no variation or shadow of turning." (James 1:17)

I love the imagery in this promise. There is not even a hint or a small shadow to indicate that God has changed His mind about loving and blessing you. Take to heart what the Lord said through the prophet: *"For I am the Lord, I do not change."* (Malachi 3:6) Read these passages out loud until you make them a part of your belief system. Say it now, "He's the giver of good and perfect gifts." He isn't handing out scorpions, snakes and stones. He is lovingly giving you good and perfect gifts. That's who He is and that is what He does. As He has done it for others, He will do it for you. Believe it and receive it! Then give Him praise, glory, honor, and majesty for all the good and perfect gifts He has given to you as well as all those He has faithfully promised to give you in the future! It makes me want to shout, "Hallelujah! Thank you Father God! You are so good! You are good all the time."

If you want to know God's will, study His Word, pray and ask! He is faithful! He will give you all you need! He will answer when you call! When you truly seek, He will make sure you find what you need. Never give up! Keep pressing in until you receive what you need and what others need to know through your ministry. I want to release the prayer below to you and on your behalf. Read it aloud with an emphasis on knowing the will of God. Pray it over yourself and use it in your intercessory prayers for others. It is solidly based on the will of God and anchored in the everlasting Word of God. Use it often to open the storehouse of heaven so that Father God can pour out blessings beyond what you can contain. Amen!

"For this reason we also, since the day we heard it, do not cease to pray for you, and to ask that you may

*be filled with the **knowledge of His will** in all wisdom and spiritual understanding; that you may walk worthy of the Lord, fully pleasing Him, being fruitful in every good work and increasing in the knowledge of God"* (Colossians 1:9-10)

THE GUIDE BOOK TO GOD'S WILL

Check it out for yourself. Over and over in passage after passage you can read in the Bible powerful statements based on the promise: "this is the will of God." When I provided this training in Chicago, Pastor Huh Chul rushed out of the room, looked it up on his computer Bible, and found 312 references to the will of God. Try it for yourself. Print out all those powerful statements and use them in your prayers and with you intercessory prayer team. Working your way through that list should give you plenty to pray about for a long time. Here is another example of praying the will of God given by Paul:

"Rejoice always, pray without ceasing, in everything give thanks; for this is the will of God in Christ Jesus for you." (1 Thessalonians 5:16-18)

According to this passage of scripture, what is God's will for you, your family, your church, and your prayer team? It is God's will for you to rejoice always, and He is ready to do what it takes to put that joy into your heart. You can count on Him to answer prayers that give you so much joy that it spills over into praise for Him. The Lord wills for you to pray constantly, and He motivates you to do that by being ever present to answer your prayers and provide what you need as well as what you are asking for others. Trust Him! He is your source, and He is faithful at all times. The third thing Paul identifies as the will of God is for you to give thanks to the Lord in everything. Why would you do that? Because in all things, you see that He is working for your good. We know He works for our good, because He is also an intercessor warrior on our behalf. Paul clearly knew this when He wrote to the church in Rome.

> *"Now He who searches the hearts knows what the mind of the Spirit is, because He makes intercession for the saints <u>according to the will of God</u>. And we know that all things work together for good to those who love God, to those who are the called according to His purpose."* (Romans 8:27-28)

Now, that's not too difficult is it? As some comedians imitating old-time country preachers say: "It's in the book!" But here is the problem: it's in the book. Where should it be? It should be in your heart. How do you get it there? Just like David, you meditate on it day and night. You say it over and over aloud, until it resides in your heart and in your mind. You need to study it, confess it, receive it, and make it your own. When you practice this, you will truly experience a renewal of your mind. Soon your first thought will be a direct reference to what the Word of God says about the will of God.

> *"And do not be conformed to this world, but be transformed by the renewing of your mind, that you may* prove what is *that good and acceptable and <u>perfect will of God</u>."* (Romans 12:2)

The renewal of the mind is not a destination. You are never really able to say that you have arrived. It is a journey you undertake, and a process you choose. You don't wake up one morning and say, "Well that's it! I know all that I need to know. I don't need to study the Word of God anymore, because I've got it and understand it all." I am sorry, but it just doesn't work that way. No matter how many times you go through the Word of God, there is more that He can and will release to you if you obediently seek, ask and knock. For me, this is an exciting thought and a wonderful promise. I love all the discoveries I make along the journey. Every day He provides something new and more exciting than the day before.

When you approach your journey into the Word with expectancy and enthusiasm, you will find what you seek. When you find it or more properly when you are found by Him and His truth, you will discover the truth about His *"good and acceptable and perfect will!"* It is after all, the journey you undertook when you decided to go deeper and deeper into His perfect Word and Will.

When you develop this as a life pattern, it will become natural for you to think first of Him, because you know that this is His Will for you. Then you will be motivated from deep within to pray for the perfect will of God. When you're walking in His will, you naturally pray His will. When you live for His will to be done on earth, you pray it. When your life goal is to please Him, He walks with you. This is His will for you!

IMAGINE HAVING THE POWER BEHIND GOD'S WILL

I am convinced that there is no real mystery here. God has made himself known in His Word, and He has revealed volumes of information about His will. Will you have to work to find it? Yes! But, the work itself will produce so much fruit in your life, strength in your spirit, and comfort to your soul. I would like to challenge you to a lifetime of dedicated Bible study. God has provided all you need. You just need to get into the Word and seek it. If the amount of material in the Bible seems to overwhelm you, remember that God is bigger than all of it and His plan for you is greater than can be contained in all the books in the world.

"This is the disciple who testifies of these things, and wrote these things; and we know that his testimony is true. And there are also many other things that Jesus did, which if they were written one by one, I suppose that even the world itself could not contain the books that would be written. Amen." (John 21:24-25)

When you make the decision to explore the entire Bible to learn more about Father God and His plans, the task may see too large at that moment for you to accomplish all of it. You may wonder how you will ever comprehend the mind of God. You never will know all there is to know about Him, but I want to assure you that there is no real mystery in what He provides for you? Remember that in the New Testament the word mystery actually means something formerly hidden which has now been made manifest.

Here is one of those great and wonderful truths about the Lord. God wants everyone to see Jesus and in knowing Him to be raised to eternal life with Him. Father God has graciously entrusted the task of helping people to see Jesus to you and me. When people see Jesus and believe in Him through your witness, you can boldly proclaim, "Mission accomplished!" However, the job is not done. After the battle has been won and the enemy has been vanquished, it is time to do nation building. Our ultimate goal is to "make disciples of all nations." During this time of building up the kingdom of God, we are called of the Lord to continue as His witnesses and to always intercede for those He is seeking to save.

Just saying you are an intercessor warrior doesn't make you one. This is a special calling from the Lord and requires an anointing from Him. You must have the anointing in order to receive the impartation of His authority needed to accomplish your part of the mission. Jesus gives us a very sobering thought about our relationship with Him. To be His, you must know Him and receive your call from Him.

"Not everyone who says to Me, 'Lord, Lord,' shall enter the kingdom of heaven, but he who does the will of My Father in heaven. Many will say to Me in that day, 'Lord, Lord, have we not prophesied in Your name, cast out demons in Your name, and done many wonders in Your name?' And then I will declare to them, 'I never knew you; depart from Me, you who practice lawlessness!'" (Matthew 7:21-23)

Responding to the call of the Lord to be a warrior is a life time challenge. We all need spiritual support from other intercessors to be empowered to succeed. Even anointed intercessors need to have people dedicated to praying for them. The Apostle Paul often asked the churches to pray for him to have the strength to persevere to the end. Peter needed the support of the early church interceding for him in prison. We are not called to do the job alone. That's why Jesus puts us into teams. That's why He established the power of agreement. He did it so we will learn to intercede for each other, and realize that we need one another.

Do you have an intercessory team behind you and your ministry? Are they covering you with prayer as you do the work of the kingdom? Do you feel a need for that kind of support? If you do, I have some "Great News!" You have two really powerful intercessors lined up as the first members of your team. The Lord Jesus constantly intercedes for you with the Father.

"Because of this oath, Jesus has become the guarantee of a better covenant. Now there have been many of those priests, since death prevented them from continuing in office; but because Jesus lives forever, he has a permanent priesthood. Therefore he is able to save completely those who come to God through him, because he always lives to intercede for them." (Hebrews 7:22-25)

Just when you think it can't possibly get any better than this, you recall that the Holy Spirit also intercedes for you. In addition, He releases His prayers with your prayers when you pray in the Spirit. This is one of the reasons it is so important for every believer to have a prayer language. This method of praying is critically important for intercessor warriors.

"Now He who searches the hearts knows what the mind of the Spirit is, because He makes intercession for the saints according to the will of God." (Romans 8:27)

How does the Holy Spirit intercede? First, He intercedes according to the will of God. Next, He has an intimate knowledge of our lives. He knows us in spirit, soul, and body. He knows us better than we know ourselves. He remembers things about us which we have forgotten or repressed. This is another reason why it is so important for intercessors to be Spirit led.

You must build your intercessor warrior spirit on these precious foundation stones.

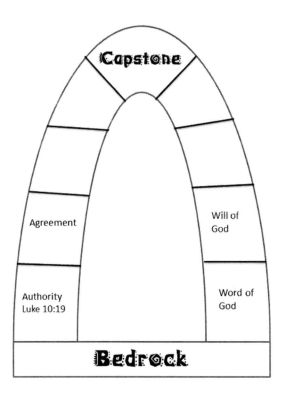

Will of God: The Fourth Stone in the Foundation

CHAPTER 5

THE STONE OF PERSISTENCE

During the writing of this chapter, the Lord gave me a vision about persistence in prayer. I wrote it in my journal and sent it out by email to a few friends. The next few paragraphs appear as I wrote them in the journal of my Third Heaven experiences.

"I closed my eyes as I went down on my knees and bowed before the Lord in worship. Immediately, I was given a very simple but elegant vision of someone on their knees praying in front of a small stained glass window. At first I thought this was a woman with a shawl over her head praying. The light coming through the stained glass in the window was bathing her with rich and warm colors. It seemed that the Lord was releasing something into her as the light poured over her.

As I went face down before the Lord, I was lifted up to the open portal into heaven. This morning, I was allowed to watch something marvelous happening in the portal. The opening into Heaven kept changing shapes while symbols in those same shapes appeared in the opening. It was very interesting to watch, but I realized that I did not really understand what was happening. I asked the Holy Spirit to help me understand. I didn't hear a voice, but I suddenly felt like I knew what this meant. Each of the shapes in the opening and the symbols appearing in the center of it appealed to people from different parts of the world. When the shapes and symbols changed, an appeal was going out to a different group of people. Then I heard the Lord say, 'I am drawing people from all around the world to come into my presence!'

A scripture came into my mind at that time. *'Draw near to God and He will draw near to you. Cleanse your hands, you sinners; and purify your hearts, you double-minded.'* (James 4:8) When I first looked at this verse, the second part seemed like a rebuke. However, this morning I understood that it was an offer of grace to those who are willing to ascend to be with the Lord. I remembered Psalm 23:3-6:

> *"Who may ascend into the hill of the Lord? Or who may stand in His holy place? He who has clean hands and a pure heart, who has not lifted up his soul to an idol, nor sworn deceitfully. He shall receive blessing from the Lord, and righteousness from the God of his salvation. This is Jacob, the generation of those who seek Him, who seek Your face.'*

Rather than giving a rebuke, James wanted people to know that the Lord is calling on His people to make the preparations necessary in order to draw near to Him. We need to cleanse our hands and purify our hearts. To do this, we need an outpouring of His grace. God has already provided that as well. My thoughts went back to verse six in James chapter four, *"But He gives more grace. Therefore He says: 'God resists the proud, but gives grace to the humble.'"* The Lord is providing everything you need to draw near to Him, but it is up to you to willingly receive it.

Suddenly, I was lifted up to the throne room in heaven. Except for me, it was vacant. I don't remember seeing this before. I was puzzled and wondered what I should do. Then it came to me. I knelt down to worship and praise the Lord. Then

I went face down in the soft warm gold dust on the floor of heaven. All I wanted to do in that moment was worship Him. Suddenly the vision of the person praying before the stained glass window came back. There was more light in the room this time and I could see that the person had a prayer shawl on their head and over their shoulders and arms. I realized that I was not able to determine if it was a man or a woman, because this message is for both.

The Spirit helped me to understand that the person praying under the stained glass window was extremely persistent in prayer. It didn't matter how long it took for the answer to manifest, this person was going to stay at it in prayer. The Lord said, 'Not many people are persistent any more. If they don't get instant results, they give up and go away offended. I can't really honor that kind of prayer!' I sensed a note of sadness in the voice of the Lord. It was clear that He wanted to answer more prayers, but impatience and offense blocked people from receiving His answers.

On a scale of one to ten (ten being the highest) how persistent are you? How long will you stick with it in prayer? May we become people who will stand in faith as long as it takes! May we anchor our trust in Him and know that He is with us and will bless us! May we trust Him to do all things in His timing rather than ours! May we become persistent prayer warriors! Amen and Amen!

I looked again to James, chapter four and my eyes focused on verse ten, '*Humble yourselves in the sight of the Lord, and He will lift you up.*' Hallelujah! Thank you, Lord, for your faithfulness unto us and for inviting us to draw near to you!"

In past generations, people have held to the notion that patience is a virtue. But today people seem to believe that it a necessary evil which you often have to endure in order to get what you want. We have built systems and procedures to make sure that we receive everything we want quickly and easily. If it takes a long time, many people will just give up. It is as if everything which doesn't happen instantly is not going to happen at all. I remember an experience I had during my military service. I was the chaplain for a basic training unit and had spiritual coverage for a large number of new soldiers. During this time, I was not responsible for the soldiers in the Reception Station which was located nearby. However when the assigned chaplain was away, the leaders there sent some of the people to me for counseling. I am sharing one of my experiences with these newly arriving soldiers. However, it is also representative of many similar situations I dealt with during that tour of duty.

A young soldier rushed into my office to explain why he needed to be released from the army immediately. He told a very long and detailed story about all his attempts to adjust and cope with the pressure of military service. He told me about several instances where leaders in his unit had talked him into trying again and how he had done this over and over again. But, now he knew that it was never going to work and he had to get out of the army right now. I was finally able to get a word into the conversation. This was such a long detailed story that I wondered how long he had been at the base. To my surprise, he looked at his watch instead of his calendar. Then he said, "I have been here for over three hours now! How can they expect me to do any more than I've already done?" Before we could get into the discussion, he had one other really big concern. If he got out today, would he still get his benefits? Would the army still pay for four years of college?

When the young recruit began the story and regaled me with all his attempts to stick with it, I listened carefully to the stories which he thought reflected great persistence on his part. It is sometimes amazing to see just how little some people know about persistence. It is equally amazing to see how quickly people give up and quit. How persistent are you? How long do you stick with your prayers and faith before you decide to give in and give up? When I am asked about how long we should pray for something to manifest, my answer is always the same: "As long as it takes!" As I considered the question about what kind of persistence the Lord desires, my thoughts went to the story of someone who demonstrated extraordinary persistence and courage.

"From the Jews five times I received forty stripes minus one. Three times I was beaten with rods; once I was stoned; three times I was shipwrecked; a night and a day I have been in the deep; in journeys often, in perils of waters, in perils of robbers, in perils of my own countrymen, in perils of the Gentiles, in perils in the city, in perils in the wilderness, in perils in the sea, in perils among false brethren; in weariness and toil, in sleeplessness often, in hunger and thirst, in fastings often, in cold and nakedness—besides the other things, what comes upon me daily: my deep concern for all the churches." (2 Corinthians 11:24-28)

Now, this is an inspirational story about persistence. It is difficult to imagine all of that coming upon one disciple of Jesus Christ. Yet, we know it is true. Most people would have quit long before this. Most men and women would have given up at some point along the way. What faith and courage it must have taken for Paul to endure all of this for the gospel of Jesus Christ! Now, the really impressive thing is found in that last statement. As he endured all of this, his real struggle was his *"deep concern for all the churches."* Unlike the other things Paul endured, this deep concern was a burden he carried every day. Can you imagine the power of his intercessory prayers based on this level of commitment and concern?

INTERCESSOR MUST STAND ON A FIRM FOUNDATION

"Those from among you shall build the old waste places; You shall raise up the foundations of many generations; And you shall be called the Repairer of the Breach, The Restorer of Streets to Dwell In." (Isaiah 58:12)

The Lord not only tells us to stand on authority, but Jesus modeled it when He began His ministry by establishing HIS AUTHORITY. He said, *"All things have been delivered to Me by My Father"* (Matthew 11:27a,) Immediately after the wilderness temptation, Jesus gave His first sermon in the synagogue. Before He began to speak He read from the book of Isaiah.

"The Spirit of the Lord is upon Me, because He has anointed Me to preach the gospel to the poor; He has sent Me to heal the brokenhearted, to proclaim liberty to the captives and recovery of sight to the blind, to set at liberty those who are oppressed; to proclaim the acceptable year of the Lord." (Luke 4:18-19, [Isa 61:1-2]) *"Today this Scripture is fulfilled in your hearing."* (Luke 4:21)

The first sentence of His sermon was a declaration of His authority as God's anointed servant. He declared that He had been given authority to preach, heal, liberate, and proclaim. Jesus firmly placed His foot on the stone of authority before beginning the work Father God had given Him.

Next, Jesus firmly placed the other foot on the stone of God's Word. In fact, Jesus based all of His words and work on the WORD OF GOD. He is a role model for us when we step into our calling to be disciples and serve as intercessor warriors for the kingdom of God. In the same way Jesus always did what He saw the Father doing, it is our task to do what we see Jesus doing and to say what we hear Him saying. Remember that Jesus overcame the works of Satan with the Word of God.

"Then Jesus said to him, 'Away with you, Satan! For it is written, ""You shall worship the Lord your God, and Him only you shall serve.""'" (Matthew 4:10)

Jesus used the Word of God as the basis of His commission, and it is a foundation stone for our work and service to the Lord. Are you standing on the foundation of the Word of God? If not, it is time to restore the foundations.

Jesus not only taught about agreeing with others in prayer, He also modeled the appropriate behavior. He consistently worked in accordance within the LAW OF AGREEMENT. He was always in agreement with His Father.

"Then Jesus answered and said to them, 'Most assuredly, I say to you, the Son can do nothing of Himself, but what He sees the Father do; for whatever He does, the Son also does in like manner.'" (John 5:19)

Everything Jesus did and everything Jesus said was in agreement with the Father. This was such a foundational principle with Jesus that He could say, *"I and My Father are one."* (John 10:30) That is precisely why the power of God was present in His intercession.

Jesus was intimately aware of what Father God wanted Him to do. Therefore, He prayed and acted according to GOD'S WILL.

"He went a little farther and fell on His face, and prayed, saying, 'O My Father, if it is possible, let this cup pass from Me; nevertheless, not as I will, but as You will.'" (Matthew 26:39)

Jesus knew God's will and this is a prayer of submission. Jesus knew His purpose and the power behind God's will.

"Then I said, 'Behold, I have come — in the volume of the book it is written of Me — to do Your will, O God.'" (Hebrews 10:7

THE FIFTH STONE IN THE FOUNDATION IS PERSISTENCE

Remembering that *"faith comes by hearing and hearing by the Word of God"* (Romans 10:17) I urge you to continue the practice of reading scriptures aloud. This will help you in several ways. You use more of your five senses in doing this. You see it and hear it. This effectively doubles your opportunity and ability to remember. Every time you read it, you are building up the memory of these words in your mind. You will remember more from a voice you trust, and the voice you trust the most is your own. Let your spirit and soul hear you read aloud Luke 18:1-8:

"Then He spoke a parable to them, that men always ought to pray and not lose heart, saying: 'There was in a certain city a judge who did not fear God nor regard man. Now there was a widow in that city; and she came to him, saying, "'Get justice for me from my adversary.'" And he would not for a while; but afterward he said within himself, "'Though I do not fear God nor regard man, yet because this widow troubles me I will avenge her, lest by her continual coming she weary me.'" Then the Lord said, 'Hear what the unjust judge said. And shall God not avenge His own elect who cry out day and night to Him, though He bears long with them? I tell you that He will avenge them speedily. Nevertheless, when the Son of Man comes, will He really find faith on the earth?'" (Luke 18:1-8)

JESUS CONNECTS PERSISTENCE WITH TRUE FAITH

"True faith" is the kind of faith which helped the disciples to prepare themselves for the outpouring of the Holy Spirit on the Day of Pentecost. This is the kind of faith which prompts true disciples today to be constantly in prayer.

"These all continued with one accord in prayer and supplication, with the women and Mary the mother of Jesus, and with His brothers." (Acts 1:14)

Do you want the Promise of the Father? Pray constantly! Do you want the results the disciples got, then you must be ready to do what they did. Paul taught the church in Roman to imitate his prayer life. The number one thing he references is that he was persistent in prayer.

"For God is my witness, whom I serve with my spirit in the gospel of His Son, that without ceasing I make mention of you always in my prayers." (Romans 1:9)

Do you want the power of God in your life? Pray constantly! Paul gave great pastoral advice to his spiritual son Timothy. He wanted Timothy to know that he was always with him in prayer and that he could always count on him to continue to do so. Timothy was wise enough to imitate Paul who was imitating Jesus.

"I thank God, whom I serve with a pure conscience, as my forefathers did, as without ceasing I remember you in my prayers night and day," (2 Timothy 1:3)

Do you want to be an intercessor? Be ready and willing to pray constantly! Do you want to be someone others can count on to pray fervently and constantly for them? Then practice praying constantly! Father God is always looking for people who are willing to intercede for others? Will He find that willingness in you? Isaiah gives a word from the Lord which is very sad. In this verse you can sense the true heart of God.

"He (God) saw that there was no man, and wondered that there was no intercessor; Therefore His own arm brought salvation for Him; and His own righteousness, it sustained Him. (Isaiah 59:16)

Over and over, we see the power of the Holy Spirit being released at just the right moment in response to the urgent plea of believers. After the resurrection of Jesus, He directed them to go to Jerusalem and wait for power to come on them. They prayed constantly and in unity for ten days. I believe they would have prayed longer if it was necessary They were ready to pray as long as it took to see His power manifest in their lives and work. They were hungry and thirsty to receive all God had for them and they persisted until it came. Do you want it badly enough to pray for ten days? Maybe you will have to pray longer. How long are you willing to wait on the promise of God and continue to stand in faith, praying constantly?

So many of the people I know pray a few quick prayers and then look around to see if anything happened. They are not going by faith. They are only going by what they can see. When they don't see immediate results, they quit. Isn't this the description of a "double-minded person?" What should a double minded person expect to receive? James says that they should expect nothing.

"So I sought for a man among them who would make a wall, and stand in the gap before Me on behalf of the land, that I should not destroy it; but I found no one." (Ezekiel 22:30)

When the Lord looks again for an intercessor, will He find one in you? Will He find one in me? I would like to think so, but it will not happen unless we become intentional about our intercessory prayers. It will not happen unless we model and teach persistence in prayer. It will not happen unless we are people of faith who will take a stand for the Lord and keep on standing as long as it takes.

"Therefore take up the whole armor of God, that you may be able to withstand in the evil day, and having done all, to stand. Stand therefore," (Ephesians 6:13-14a)

PERSISTENCE AND CONSTANCY DEMONSTRATE FAITH

"For the eyes of the Lord run to and fro throughout the whole earth, to show Himself strong on behalf of those whose heart is loyal to Him." (2 Chronicles 16:9a)

Who among us today has a loyal heart? The Lord is looking for someone who will be able to receive what He wants to give. He wants to show Himself strong on our behalf, but He is waiting for people who are able to receive it and willing to stand for it. He is looking for people who will not give up, but will continue to pray through everything which comes against the Lord.

Jesus noticed that people were giving up too quickly. He chose to teach them by using a parable. Luke makes His purpose clear to the readers. Jesus wanted to teach people to pray without ever choosing to give up. That is Jesus heart for you and me. It is the kind of heart and commitment He is seeking from those He calls and anoints to be intercessor warriors. If He came today, would He find faith in your heart? Would He find someone who has made a commitment to persist in prayer as long as it takes?

> *"Then Jesus told his disciples a parable to show them that they should always pray and not give up."* (Luke 18:1, NIV)

What kind of faith is involved in quickly giving up? It certainly is not saving faith or the faith to heal. It is not the kind of faith we read about in Hebrews 11:1, *"Now faith is the substance of things hoped for, the evidence of things not seen."* Many people who believe that Jesus did all these wonderful miracles, healings, signs and wonders in the past simply do not believe it can happen today. They certainly do not believe it will happen for them or through them. That takes us back to Jesus' penetrating question:

> *"Nevertheless, when the Son of Man comes, will He really find faith on the earth?"* (Luke 18:8b)

In the absence of faith, Jesus can do little in our lives. One of the few things which truly amazed Jesus was the lack of faith among people who claimed to be believers, leaders, and teachers of God's Word. The situation has not changed much in the last two thousand years. Church going people do not fully understand or truly believe the power of God available to them and the church today. Since they don't see it or believe it, none of it is available in their ministries.

> *"He could not do any miracles there, except lay his hands on a few sick people and heal them. And he was amazed at their lack of faith."* (Mark 6:5)

There are several ways I would like to amaze Jesus, but having a lack of faith is not one of them. How about you? You may ask, "So, what can we do about it? How can we build up our faith?" The Bible teaches us many ways to do this. We are told to stir up our faith and watch God work wonders. How do you stir up your faith? There are so many examples in the Bible. I am especially drawn to the Psalms and read about how David practiced the art of stirring up his faith in God. He would begin to remember all the victories the Lord had helped him to win. He remembered when God saved him from imminent danger. He remembered when the Lord protected him from Saul's attempts to kill him. As he reminded himself of these victories from the Lord, his faith grew stronger and stronger. Some of the most desperate Psalms end with decrees about the blessing, favor, and salvation of the Lord. What changed? David changed as he remember God's faithfulness in the past and put his trust back in the Lord to be faithful in the present as well as in the future.

You can follow David's example and stir up your memories of what God has done for you in the past. Remember and speak out loud about times when He has protected you and brought you out of trouble. Remember how he comforted you in the night and reassured you of the joy which would come in the morning. Remember his promises to help you and save you from trouble and danger. Watch faith welling up inside you again. Take confidence in the Lord who has always been there for you and will never leave you or abandon you.

You can read the grand promises in the Scriptures about what the Lord plans for you and what He plans for the future of all believers. As you read the promises over and over, they get anchored in your soul and your faith is lifted up. We could all use a faith lift from time to time. Perhaps this is your day. Remember all the times when the Lord has answered your prayers in the past and have faith that you can always count on Him.

Paul saw that Timothy had a *"genuine faith"* which had been handed down by his mother and grandmother. This is an exciting idea. We can hand down our faith to our children and grandchildren. How did that happen for Timothy? They obviously told him many times about how God was faithful in protecting and caring for them. They shared stories with Timothy which assured him that he could always put his trust in his faithful and loving Father God. You can do that for your family as well. Constantly remind them with real examples of how the Lord has been faithful in the past and encourage them to have faith in Him for their future. Encourage them to stir up their faith more and more. That is what Paul advised Timothy to do. Build on the foundation of faith which has already been laid down for you.

> *"When I call to remembrance the genuine faith that is in you, which dwelt first in your grandmother Lois and your mother Eunice, and I am persuaded is in you also. Therefore I remind you to stir up the gift of God which is in you through the laying on of my hands."* (2 Timothy 1:5-6)

Remember His faithfulness and then stir up your faith. It is not enough to just be aware of and remember what the Lord has done for others. You have to make it your own. You do that by remembering your own history with God, and then you increase it by stirring it up in your heart until it becomes the substance of things hoped for. It requires real persistence to do this and that is God's calling and promise to you. Stir up your faith and then stir up an attitude of persistence.

TRUE INTERCESSOR WARRIORS DON'T QUIT

> *"And let us not grow weary while doing good, for in due season we shall reap if we do not lose heart."* (Galatians 6:9)

You must learn to trust God for the harvest. We often hear this in terms of harvests for financial resources, but it goes well beyond that. We sow seeds into the hearts of people as we plant testimonies about Jesus into their souls. We sow our time and our talents into others as we patiently and persistently mentor them toward becoming true disciples of Jesus Christ. Be persistent and trust God for the harvest. Of course this does also apply to financial seeds which we sow into the kingdom to help spread the gospel around the world. Good harvests result from planting much. How are you doing with your planting?

"But this I say: He who sows sparingly will also reap sparingly, and he who sows bountifully will also reap bountifully. So let each one give as he purposes in his heart, not grudgingly or of necessity; for God loves a cheerful giver. And God is able to make all grace abound toward you, that you, always having all sufficiency in all things, may have an abundance for every good work."
(2 Corinthians 9:6-8)

Good harvests result from waiting for things to grow while getting ready for the time of reaping. This requires patience and persistence. I have always loved gardening. When I first began to sow seeds, I wanted to see results quickly. I went out every day to see if the seeds had sprouted and if they had been able to break through the surface of the soil. At one point, I decided to help them. I began to open up the soil above them to make it easier for them, but this resulted in a disaster for the little plants. They needed to force their way through the crust on the ground to peel away the remnants of the seed covering. When this didn't happen because of my interference, the plants were unable to break through on their own and fulfill their destiny. If we want to be harvesters in the fields of the Lord, we must learn patience and allow those we help to push their own way through, and stir up their own faith.

If you truly want to have an abundant harvest, you need to expectantly prepare yourselves to receive it. After the time of sowing, there are some things you can and should do while you wait for your harvest to come in. You must invest time and energy into watering and nourishing those seeds you have sown in people who follow your leadership. You need to spend a great deal of time lifting up intercessory prayers in order to release the power of God in your area of authority. You can trust the Lord. Your intercessory prayers will help others to be built up, strengthened, comforted, and nourished by the living Bread of Heaven, Jesus the Christ.

In times of waiting for the harvest, intercessors can build up their own faith. One of the very powerful ways to do this is through praise and worship.

"Sing praise to the Lord, you saints of His, and give thanks at the remembrance of His holy name." (Psalm 30:4)

Your praise songs not only lift up your worship to the Lord, but they also lift up your spirit as you remind yourself of God's faithfulness. Praising the Lord helps you to remember how he has guided you in the past and how He has always given you victory in every time of battle. Remembering these previous victories helps you to build up your *"most holy faith."* In the praise songs, you are reminded of "His holy name" and the awesome power released every time you speak it aloud. When you speak that name reverently in your praise, enemy strongholds begin to crumble and every argument and high thing established against Him is brought low. When you worship in spirit and in truth, you release great grace, great faith, great miracles, and awesome signs, and wonders.

In times of waiting, warriors build up their expectancy. When they become cheerleaders for the other warriors, they help to lift their own spirits and increase their own faith in

God. In the process of giving the testimonies of Jesus, they release prophetic words which help others at the same time as they build up, encourage, and strengthen themselves. Jesus told people that they could receive what they expected — what they believed would happen. If the Roman Centurion had not expected his servant to be healed, he would not have been healed. If the blind man had not expected to receive his sight, he would have been blind all his life. What do you expect? Build up the level of your expectancy.

Don't let the problems and difficulties which come your way deter you. Don't let sorrow and loss steal your joy. Remember God's word and break the power of every oppressive spirit sent against you. Remember and speak aloud the words of Psalm 30:5b, *"Weeping may endure for a night, but joy comes in the morning."*

It may be tough now, but don't give up! Joy is coming! The night may seem long and the answer may appear to be far away. Don't give up! The night is almost over and the joy of the Lord will soon return to your spirit. No one else can truly know what you are going through right now. You may be enduring some intense pain, deep feelings of loss, or some great heaviness in your spirit. But take heart! You can trust God! He is faithful. In the worst part of the dark nights of your soul, remember the faithfulness of God. Let your faith build up as you persist in trusting your faithful Father God. It may seem hopeless to the world, but not to you. You are expecting things to change in the morning. You are expecting the joy of the Lord to return and blessings and favor to be released to you.

In the hearts of real warriors, faith and hope replace fears and doubts every time. Real warriors say, "Give up? You must be kidding! Just before dawn? Give up just before my miracle? No way!"

I can't speak for the rest of the world! I can't speak for the entire church! I can't speak for you. I can only speak for me and my faith, and you are the only one who can speak to your own faith. But this I affirm: "When He comes, He will find faith in this heart of mine!" I encourage you to make this confession over and over until it is anchored in your heart. Keep speaking it with your spiritual authority until it becomes substance! Persist in prayer until all the answers and promises manifest in your life and ministry! Amen!

INTERCESSOR-WARRIORS BELIEVE JESUS

"Most assuredly, I say to you, he who believes in Me, the works that I do he will do also; and greater works than these he will do, because I go to My Father." (John 14:12)

I am convinced that most people who say they are Christians don't really believe what Jesus said in this passage. They may believe He said it, but they don't necessarily believe that it is true. They don't really live in a way that validates their faith in this powerful affirmation. I have heard this over and over. These people are convinced that Jesus didn't really mean what He seems to have said. They twist the words around in all sorts of ways to disprove this Word from the Lord. I've heard all kinds of lame excuses for the lack of power in the church today. Some say, "When Jesus said this what He really meant was that all of us combined could preach the gospel to more people." But, that is not what He said. He didn't speak about large groups or about preaching. Jesus clearly spoke it in the singular — *"He who believes in Me. . ."*

I want to give you an important kingdom principle: If you have to twist the words of Jesus to fit your belief system, it is time to change what you believe and get back on the foundation established through Jesus Christ. If you find yourself quoting other people (even people in the Bible) to disprove what Jesus said, you need to drop those beliefs and study once again what the Lord said. No other foundation can be established than that which has already been laid down for you in Jesus. He is the cornerstone many builders have rejected to the peril of their own souls. Don't be one of them. Get back on the sure foundation and take your stand with Jesus.

Other doubters say that these words and prayers of Jesus were only for the original twelve apostles. They believe that the time for these things to operate in the church ended a long time ago, and we have been left without authority and power. However, these ideas simply do not hold water. These manmade theories and doctrines are often blatantly contrary to the teaching of the Bible. The New Testament mentions many people who well into the second and third generation of believers were still doing these things. Numerous miracles, signs and wonders, and healings are referenced in the stories about disciples who were not among the original twelve.

Are you one of those who truly believes Jesus? Do you believe that the words Jesus spoke were true then and are still true today? Do you truly believe in Him? Do you believe He meant what He said? I believe Him! Jesus himself gives us the reason "why" God does these healings, signs and wonders in the ministry of faithful believers.

"By this My Father is glorified, that you bear much fruit; so you will be My disciples." (John 15:8)

God isn't glorified by a bunch of weak, sick, tired, poor and doubting followers. God isn't glorified by prayers that aren't answered. God is glorified by the fruit of our labors for Him. God is glorified in the powerful works of His people. Healings, miracles, signs, and wonders all confirm the truth and efficacy of His Word along with all the content of the gospel of the kingdom. To fully receive this and operate at the level of faith Jesus is speaking of, we have to give up years of religious training, false teachings, doctrines of man, and the deception of the enemy.

"But know this, that in the last days perilous times will come: For men will be lovers of themselves, lovers of money, boasters, proud, blasphemers, disobedient to parents, unthankful, unholy, unloving, unforgiving, slanderers, without self-control, brutal, despisers of good, traitors, headstrong, haughty, lovers of pleasure rather than lovers of God, having a form of godliness but denying its power. And from such people turn away!" (2 Timothy 3:1-5)

We should not be surprised when these things happen. Our faith should not be shaken by people who rise up in rebellion against the Lord and teach false things. We should not be surprised by the false words coming from false prophets and false teachers. The Lord told us this would happen. Paul told Timothy that it would happen. John told all the believers that it would happen. Peter warned about it in his two letters to the church. No more surprises! We know the enemy and understand his tactics. He is doing the same thing today that he did in the Garden of Eden, and he will still be doing it tomorrow. Don't let him fool you with high sounding but false words!

I want you to know that Satan is not threatened by people going to many of these churches. Satan loves the religious spirit which is influencing and controlling many churches. He loves the religious spirit which still remains to some degree in most of us. This is the spirit that says you will be okay with God if you just go to church, be nice, and don't expect anything to happen. When the church teaches these manmade false doctrines, Satan can just relax and watch the veil of deception come down over our eyes and ears. He doesn't have to do much against us because we do it to ourselves.

Remember that it was the "religious people" controlled by a religious spirit who killed Jesus. He was too radical about holding to the truth of the scriptures. As a result, He upset their system of self-made rules, rituals and excuses. He exposed their false teaching, manmade doctrines, and fleshly systems of belief. He confronted people with their hypocrisy and offered them a better way. He offered for them to break free from religion and once again step up on the foundation stones established by the Lord long ago. He offered them the way of faith.

Will Jesus find any faith when He returns? Will His people persist in maintaining their trust in Him? Will His true church continue to hold on to the pure teachings of the gospel of the kingdom? We need to keep making our affirmations of faith and allegiance. Take a few moments and speak out this promise:" In this heart, Jesus will find faith when He returns!"

DON'T FALL ASLEEP ON YOUR WATCH

"And from the days of John the Baptist until now the kingdom of heaven suffers violence, and the violent take it by force." (Matthew 11:12)

Apparently, God is not looking for a bunch of mild mannered, seeker-sensitive, and politically correct wimps. We are at war and warfare is violent and bloody! Jesus made it clear that the kingdom has suffered violence, and it will continue to suffer violence. On the upside of that, real warriors are not passively sitting and waiting for someone else to do something. They are the ones who are violently pressing their way into the kingdom. They know where they belong, and they know how to press in with strength and persistence. They know the enemy and what he plans to do. They know their Lord and what He has enabled them to do in response to every attack. They will not stop until the victory is won!

"The thief does not come except to steal, and to kill, and to destroy. I have come that they may have life, and that they may have it more abundantly." (John 10:10)

The enemy only comes for these three purposes identified by Jesus. Tragically, the enemy has been successful through the centuries at stealing, killing, and destroying. But, he has only been able to do that because we are not persistently standing on our authority, the Word of God, the unity of agreement and the will of God. He took some territory. Now, it's time for the Lord's mighty warriors to take it back for the King of kings. Taking the offensive to the enemy involves some violent action. If you want to be on God's side, put on the full armor and get into the fight before it is too late!

How hard can this be? You are being asked to take your stand against an enemy who has already been defeated. Jesus came to destroy His work. On the cross, Jesus declared, "It is finished!" Jesus completed His assigned mission. He defeated the devil, death, hell and the grave. Remember Jesus' assigned mission and make it your own as you enter the fight as one of His intercessor warriors. You were called, anointed, authorized and empowered to destroy the works of the devil. It is time to get to work and win this victory for the Lord and the kingdom of God! Amen!

"He who sins is of the devil, for the devil has sinned from the beginning. For this purpose the Son of God was manifested, that He might destroy the works of the devil." (1 John 3:8)

Don't lose to a loser like Satan. Jesus already defeated him, took away all his authority, and gave that authority back to us. We need to start acting like it, and become a part of His army of mighty kingdom warriors. Are you ready to take up the challenge, pick up the gauntlet, and take the battle to the enemy?

I still hear people saying, "I just don't know what to do? What is God's plan for me? What is His will for me?" It is time to get weaned from the bottle of spiritual milk and begin to eat some adult food. Are you ready for some of the steak in the Word of God? It is time to take the challenge and accomplish your assigned kingdom mission. It is time to acknowledge your calling and your anointing. Study the teachings of Jesus. Then ask, "How much more plainly can Jesus say it?" Jesus declared: *"And I bestow upon you a kingdom, just as My Father bestowed one upon Me,"* (Luke 22:29)

If you believe Jesus, then you can believe that God bestowed a kingdom on Him. Do you believe that? If you truly believe Jesus, you have to go further than just believing that He said this. You need to receive it into your heart and live it by faith! Do you believe that a kingdom has been bestowed on you? Do you believe that you are supposed to do what you see Jesus doing? Then it is time to take action and get into the battle!

I put together some of Jesus' power statements for you. Then I added a few from some other followers of Jesus. Study them and make a decision about whether you believe Jesus or not. If you believe they are true, begin to appropriate the full meaning of these teachings into your own faith and practice. As you read and consider these faith statements, say them over and over aloud until they truly sink into your heart and become yours.

Jesus said, *"I am the light of the World."* (John 9:5, John 8:12)
Jesus said, *"you are the light of the World."* (Matthew 5:14)

Jesus said, *"I am the vine, you are the branches."* (John 15:5)

Jesus said, *"You are the salt of the earth."* (Matthew 5:13)

Jesus said, *"Destroy this temple and in three days I will raise it up."* (John 2:19)
Paul said, *"You are the temple of God."* (1 Corinthians 3:16)

Paul said, *"You are the temple of the living God."* (2 Corinthians 6:16)

Paul said, *"Now, you are the body of Christ."* (1 Corinthians 12:27)

Accepting what God says about you, is the acid test of faith! First, you need to find out what God said about you. Then, you need to decide if you can truly believe it. Can you stand on faith and believe God's calling on your life? Here is a great example. Do you really believe that you can look at yourself in a mirror and see God's glory? Before you answer read the scripture below aloud several times. Do you think it is true? If it is true, can you begin to decree it over yourself?

"But we all, with unveiled face, beholding as in a mirror the glory of the Lord, are being transformed into the same image from glory to glory, just as by the Spirit of the Lord." (2 Corinthians 3:18)

When you look in a mirror, what do you see? You may see many different things depending on where the mirror is located, but you will always see yourself! Do you know what you look like to Father God? When you look at your image in the mirror, remember that you were created in His image. When you look at yourself in the mirror, you should see someone who looks just like Jesus! You should see the same glory on you that was and is on Jesus. You should see that glory growing stronger every day. What are you seeing when you look in a mirror? Ask yourself, "Do I really believe what God is saying about me? Am I standing on faith that I am going from glory to glory by the work of the Spirit of the Lord?"

God searches for people who understand who they are in Christ. He is searching for people of faith who understand the times and know what the people of God ought to do. He is still looking for intercessor warriors who will build a wall and stand in the gap to protect His people from the wrath to come. People with very low self-esteem who believe that they are spiritually powerless cannot do these tasks effectively. When you learn what God thinks and says about His beloved children, begin to speak that over yourself.

Perhaps it's time to confess your unbelief and ask for more faith. God is raising up a generation who will stand and fight. If you're not able to do that right now, ask God for help. He is faithful to give you what you need to continue to stand!

"Therefore, since we have this ministry, as we have received mercy, we do not lose heart." (2 Corinthians 4:1)

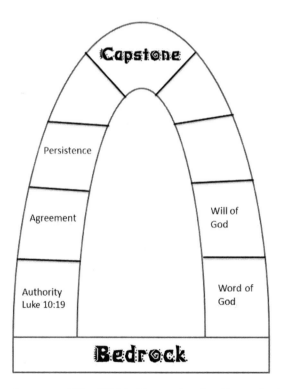

Persistence: The Fifth Stone in the Foundation

CHAPTER 6

THE STONE OF GOD'S GLORY

ஃௐ

*E*verything Jesus said and did had the primary purpose of bringing glory to the Father. We see this consistently in the prophecies about the coming of *Yeshua ha Messiach*. We see it in the things Jesus said as well as in the things He did. We learn from the Bible that all the things Jesus will do in the future will bring glory to Father God. Everything He taught also had the purpose of bringing glory to God.

Consider your own life and work. How many of the things you have said and done in the past have truly brought glory to God? Of those that did bring Him glory, how many of them happened because you made a conscious choice to accomplish that for Him? When you pray, do you first ask yourself if what you are asking Him to do will bring glory to Him? Study the life and work of Jesus with a focus on understanding what each element of His ministry on Earth had to do with bringing glory to God.

"But the end of all things is at hand; therefore be serious and watchful in your prayers. And above all things have fervent love for one another, for "love will cover a multitude of sins." Be hospitable to one another without grumbling. As each one has received a gift, minister it

to one another, as good stewards of the manifold grace of God. If anyone speaks, let him speak as the oracles of God. If anyone ministers, let him do it as with the ability which God supplies, <u>that in all things God may be glorified</u> through Jesus Christ, to whom belong the glory and the dominion forever and ever. Amen." (1 Peter 4:7-11,)

THE OUTCOMES
OF EFFECTIVE INTERCESSION

"Confess your trespasses to one another, and pray for one another, that you may be healed. The effective, fervent prayer of a righteous man avails much. Elijah was a man with a nature like ours, and he prayed earnestly that it would not rain; and it did not rain on the land for three years and six months. And he prayed again, and the heaven gave rain, and the earth produced its fruit." (James 5:16-18)

It is amazing to seriously consider that Elijah had the same nature which you and I have. He not only had the same physical nature you have, but he also had the same spiritual nature. Imagine for a moment that you are ministering under the same anointing as Elijah, and that you are able to do the things he did. Can you imagine having the authority to pray and change the weather? Imagine having enough faith in God to stand up in the presence of a large number of people and make the claim that it would not rain again until you spoke the words. Now, that is true spiritual authority which only works if God blesses it with His power.

The outcomes Elijah got from his prayers give new meaning to James 5:16, *"The effective, fervent prayer of a righteous man avails much."* Notice: this was exactly what James was clearly asserting. James attached these comments about you being in the same nature with Elijah to this affirmation about the results you should expect from your fervent intercessory prayers.

Lets look more deeply into James' assertion in the passage above. He makes a very clear and positive assertion that the *"effective, fervent prayer of a righteous man avails much!"* What does an "effective, fervent prayer" look like? It sounds much like the prayers of Epaphras which we studied early in this book. How can a prayer be effective even as it is being spoken? What would this kind of prayer sound like? I believe that this type of prayer sounds very authoritative. Are people sometimes surprised by the authority in your voice when you minister deliverance or healing? If you get this kind of response from people as you pray, you are likely praying fervent, effective, and authoritative prayers as described in the Word of God. Take a moment and reflect on the elements of this type of prayer!

First, as mentioned above, an effective prayer would have to be authoritative, but on whose authority would it be based? Reflect for a moment on all the foundation stones we have covered so far. It would have to be based on the authority God has given to the person who speaks or writes the prayer. To pray effective prayers you need to know your God given authority and work within the guidelines the Lord has given in order to release the power of God through it. Are you praying in the authority you've been given? Jesus always prayed with His God given authority. When He spoke words of healing over the sick, He did it with authority. When He cleansed the lepers, He did it with authority. When He taught, preached, prayed, and healed, it was always with authority and people notice that it was not like what others were doing. He possessed and used His authority. How about you?

Next, an effective prayer would have to be based on the Word of God. It would have to be founded on the precepts and principles of the Bible. It would have to follow the guidelines of the written, spoken, and living Word of God. Perhaps it would be a prayer which has already been written in the Bible. Or, perhaps it would be a paraphrase of one of those clearly effective prayers already provided for you in God's Word. Any prayer which is contrary to the Word of God simply will not be effective. Begin now to stop before each prayer and ask yourself: Is this in accordance with the Word of God? Look again at the prayers of Jesus and see that He always stood on this principle.

An effective prayer would also be fortified through the correct use of the law of agreement. James comments about a righteous person's prayer. In the context of this passage, we see that the elders of the church have come together in agreement. Agreement adds power to the words of a prayer and the Lord promises to honor prayers like this. If the Lord says He will answer prayers given in agreement with other believers, isn't that the very definition of "effective prayers?" An effective prayer is one which produces the desired result. Are you seeking others who will stand in agreement with you as you pray? Jesus always prayed in agreement with the Father and the Holy Spirit. He taught and modeled effective prayer for you.

Another important consideration for an effective prayer is that it must be in accordance with the known will of God. Any prayer contrary to the will of God will never be effective. However, a prayer given in accordance with the will of God already has God's power available to bring it into manifestation. Remember; you have well over 300 Biblical statements about the will of God. Check them out and make sure your prayers line up with God's desires. When you do this, you will begin to see the awesome results flowing from effective prayers. Examine yourself and see if your prayers are intentionally in agreement with the will of God. Jesus always prayed this way. Jesus didn't ask for His own will to be done. He asked that the Father's will be done on earth as it is in Heaven. In fact, He told us to pray the same way.

A fifth foundation stone for prayers to be effective is persistence. Are you willing to pray until sufficient faith arises in you to turn hope into substance? Do you persist until the thing you are praying manifests? Persistence is the foundation for effective prayer. Jesus taught this clearly in the parable of the unjust judge. The Bible says that Jesus gave this parable so that those hearing it could understand that they should never give up on their prayers.

In this current lesson, we will consider how much more effective prayers will be when the desired outcome will bring glory to God. So many prayers are self-serving. They ask the Lord to provide all the things the person giving the prayer wants for themselves. I call these types of prayer: "Gimme, Gimme prayers!" How many of your prayers are self-seeking? Some of these prayers are attempts to bring glory to the person praying. These kinds of prayers are most often spoken by those who make their own plans and then try to persuade God to help them accomplish their purposes. Prayers like this are spoken in an attempt to persuade God to bring our own will on earth rather than His.

I have listened to some people praying who only ask for things for themselves. It is a big jump for these people to learn about and move into intercessory prayer. They are just not accustomed to asking things for others unless the answers will also benefit themselves. If you are reading this book, you have most likely moved well beyond this level of prayer. You are seeking to build on the foundation given by the Lord and to increase the effectiveness of your fervent prayers. Good!

Now for another jump! Let's take this up another notch. Begin to focus on the glory of God and ask yourself what your current prayers are doing to bring glory to the Lord? As you prepare to do this, I want to pray over you with a powerful and effective prayer from the Word of God.

"And this I pray, that your love may abound still more and more in knowledge and all discernment, that you may approve the things that are excellent, that you may be sincere and without offense till the day of Christ, being filled with the fruits of righteousness which are by Jesus Christ, <u>to the glory and praise of God</u>." (Philippians 1:9-11)

I believe that all our prayers should seek outcomes which will bring glory to God! I recognize the danger of generalizations, but in the realm of spiritual truth we operate with absolutes. Meditate on this prayer Paul gave for the Philippian church. He sought many good things for them, and that is obviously the right thing to do when you are praying. Paul identifies for us his purpose in asking for these things. First, that those in the church will be filled with the fruits of righteousness which will be a powerful witness to the world. Paul identifies the source of the fruits as being Jesus Christ. Jesus was always committed to bringing glory to His Father and obviously this will accomplish that purpose. Paul joins in agreement with Jesus to affirm that the desired result is for Father God to receive glory and praise.

I challenge you to adopt a new idea and practice it regularly until it becomes an established habit. Each time you prepare to pray, start by asking yourself some important questions:

1. Do I have the authority to ask for this in prayer? If so, how shall I pray?
2. Is this in keeping with the Word of God so that I can be in agreement with Him?
3. Have I established agreement with other believers in order to increase the effectiveness of my prayers?
4. Are the things I am requesting in agreement with the known will of God?
5. Am I prepared to persist until the outcomes manifest?

6. Finally, ask yourself, will this really bring glory to God? Will it produce the fruit of righteousness resulting in the glory and praise of Father God?

Jesus modeled this type of prayer throughout His ministry on Earth and continues to do so through the work of the Holy Spirit. Jesus also taught these principles and has provided a very good working model for us:

"And when you pray, you shall not be like the hypocrites. For they love to pray standing in the synagogues and on the corners of the streets, that they may be seen by men. Assuredly, I say to you, they have their reward. But you, when you pray, go into your room, and when you have shut your door, pray to your Father who is in the secret place; and your Father who sees in secret will reward you openly. And when you pray, do not use vain repetitions as the heathen do. For they think that they will be heard for their many words." (Matthew 6:5-7)

Jesus begins by telling us not to pray in a place or in a manner which will get praise for us from others. You probably know someone who has developed a style of prayer designed to impress listeners and elicit praise from them. Remember this does not please the Father. We should pray to bring glory to God. Next, Jesus tells us to pray in the secret place we have established in our relationship with the Father. Jesus says that prayers given in secret will result in praise from God. Then Jesus cautions us to stop praying the same self-centered things over and over. The word vain means empty. Unbelievers keep praying the same empty words over and over, but never touch the heart of God because there is no substance to their words or their faith. After this brief teaching, Jesus gives the model for our prayers:

"Therefore do not be like them. For your Father knows the things you have need of before you ask Him. In this manner, therefore, pray: Our Father in heaven, Hallowed be Your name. Your kingdom come. Your will be done On earth as it is in heaven. Give us this day our daily bread. And forgive us our debts, As we forgive our debtors. And do not lead us into temptation, But deliver us from the evil one. For Yours is the kingdom and the power and the glory forever. Amen." (Matthew 6:8-13)

Look again at the second sentence in the passage above. Father God knows what you need even before you ask. Think about that! Why would you need to bring these self-centered requests up over and over? Once you are sure that the Lord knows your needs before you ask, it will change the way you pray. You will come to know with certainty that He has your best interests at heart. He has a plan for you which is to prosper you while giving you a great hope and a wonderful future in His kingdom. When you know this, your prayers get focused back on giving thanks and praise for what He has done, what He is doing, and what your faith assures you He will do in the future.

I want you to plant an idea deep in your soul and spirit so that it will be resolved once and for all. The number one focus of prayer should be the glory of God. Look again at what Paul commanded the believers in Corinth. Read it aloud until it becomes a part of the fabric of your soul and body.

"Therefore, whether you eat or drink, or whatever you do, do all to the glory of God." (1 Corinthians 10:31)

Paul takes this idea well beyond prayer. He tells us to eat in a way that brings glory to God. Drink in a manner that gives God glory. Whatever you may do today, plan to do it so that you will bring glory to God. Then ask yourself again: *How many of my prayers are intentional attempts to bring glory to God?*

"Not unto us, O Lord, not unto us, But to Your name give glory, Because of Your mercy, Because of Your truth." (Psalm 115:1)

The psalmist certainly understood this principle when he penned the passage above. I know that this is not easy for a generation of people who grew up with so many messages about always being careful to look out for "Number One" (yourself). There have been so many slogans accepted by well-meaning people which teach something opposite from the Word of God. Some examples of self center prayers follow:

"Strive to be number one in everything you do regardless of whom you must step on to get there."

Fight your way to the top!

Here is one I saw on a bumper sticker several years ago: *"He who dies with the most toys, wins!"*

This plan doesn't look like much of a victory when you see it from the Lord's perspective. For one thing you have to be dead to get your small victory. Also consider this: When you stand before the judgment seat of Christ, He will not ask you about how much money you made, how high you climbed the corporate ladder, or what awards and recognition you received. He will very likely ask you what you did to bring glory to God. What will you have to say on that day?

I want to remind you of something once again. Before you begin to pray, have you ever stopped to ask: "What can I pray to bring God glory?" Have you ever refrained from asking for something because there is no glory for God in it? Have you ever asked the Lord to teach you to pray this way?

Many people have told me that they believe Jesus Christ came just for them. On one level this sounds good. It affirms that the person has accepted what the Lord has done for them in a very personal way. On the other hand, it may be revealing something much darker. It may uncover and reveal a religious spirit which is seeking to bring glory to the one who is praying.

"For it is the God who commanded light to shine out of darkness, who has shone in our hearts to give the light of the knowledge of the glory of God in the face of Jesus Christ." (2 Corinthians 4:6)

The grammar used in this passage forces us to stop and reason within ourselves about the deeper meaning in this verse. Notice first that Christ came to bring glory to God. Then consider this. In the same way the Lord commanded light to shine out of darkness, He has commanded light to shine in your heart. This is obviously about wisdom and revelation, because the purpose of sending this into your heart is so that you can know about the glory of God and see it on the face of Jesus Christ. All of these things are gifts from God. You don't have to work these things up inside yourself. You don't have to strive more or cry out more. You just need to open up your spirit to receive all the Lord wants to pour into you.

Today, He wants to pour light into your heart so that you can see His glory and the glory of Christ Jesus. We are so blessed because our salvation brings God glory. We can't earn it. We don't deserve it. But, He freely gives it because it brings glory to Himself. Hallelujah! Thank you Lord for making us a part of this plan! Ask yourself: How brightly is the glory of the Father and the glory of Christ shining in my heart, my mind, and my prayers?

Pause for a moment and think about what kind of prayers would bring glory to God. As I have taught this in different parts of the world, I have noticed a common response to these ideas. I usually get lots of blank stares when I ask people to think of prayers which bring glory to God. They can't actually think of many of their own prayers which have given glory to

God in the past. For them, this is something completely new to consider. It is really outside their personal experience to think this way and consider how they can bring glory to God. Did you think of a prayer like this right away? Be honest! No one is looking and no one can hear what you think. People need to struggle with some of these questions to get a real grasp on this important teaching from the Word of God.

As you have been reading this chapter, perhaps you are now beginning to see some possibilities for praying this way. Remember that the Lord has given you a wonderful guide book to help you as you seek to better understand these things. You have the Bible which is like an ancient owner's manual for the human spirit, soul, and body. There are many examples of this kind of prayer in the scriptures. I pray that both you and I will be more intentional about praying to His glory!

I have some good news for you! Many of the things you are hoping for and the things you need can actually glorify God. You just need to become more focused and more intentional about it. It is truly to our benefit when we learn to pray this way. The Lord empowers and resources those who bring Him glory. When we learn to do this intentionally and effectively many more of our prayers will receive immediate answers. Again, you can turn to the prayers which are already in the Bible. Pray them over yourself and others. These prayers from the Bible are already in agreement with Him and have been designed to bring His power to bear on your situations and to result in His glory.

EFFECTIVE PRAYERS EXALT JESUS AND BRING HIM GLORY

"Therefore God also has highly exalted Him and given Him the name which is above every name, that at the name of Jesus every knee should bow, of those in heaven, and of those on earth, and of those under the

earth, and that every tongue should confess that Jesus Christ is Lord, to the glory of God the Father." (Philippians 2:9-11)

How often do you pray to exalt Jesus? In recent years, I have begun to practice this much more often. I pray for Him to be known and glorified throughout the earth. I pray that my ministry would help to make Him famous in the entire world. Do you want to take your ministry to the nations? Do you want to expand the area of your influence? Begin to pray for His glory and ask that He increase your influence to accomplish this. Can the Lord trust you to stay on course if He answers this prayer?

It is important for the Lord to be able to count on us to do what we say we will do in our ministries. It is important for the Lord to see that we are committed to being obedient servants of Jesus Christ. Here is an interesting thought: Our obedience brings glory to the Lord. There is a double impact from being obedient to pray for His glory. You and those you are praying for will receive the Lord's gifts and blessings as a means of bringing Him glory. Both things happen at the same time with the same prayers. Study the passage below and uncover this double benefit.

"But we have renounced the hidden things of shame, not walking in craftiness nor handling the word of God deceitfully, but by manifestation of the truth commending ourselves to every man's conscience in the sight of God. But even if our gospel is veiled, it is veiled to those who are perishing, whose minds the god of this age has blinded, who do not believe, lest the light of the gospel of the glory of Christ, who is the image of God, should shine on them." (2 Corinthians 4:2-4)

A changed life is a powerful testimony for the Lord. One of my seminary professors (I can't remember which one) was fond of saying: "God is changeless in that He never ceases to change!" We serve a creative God who is both changeless and constantly changing. He changes each time He develops a new or deeper relationship with one of us. He writes new songs, creates new worlds, and begins new moves in the Kingdom of God.

It is interesting that we who serve this every changing God can resist change so much. It is as if we have to admit that we have been living in error if we change an idea or slightly adjust the way we understand God. How can we possibly expect to keep up with the moves of God if we are unwilling or slow to change with Him? Most of us have a tendency to think about others when the idea of change emerges. If you want to validate this, bring up the need for people to change and ask your listeners for feedback on that idea. See how many will quickly think of ways others around them need to change. Then notice how few of the ideas have to do with the respondents' need to change.

I am going to propose a really far out idea; How about praying that you will change and that the change in you will bring glory to Father God? Do you think you can do that? Try it out and see what happens.

It has become my ambition to see every knee bow to my King of kings and Lord of lords, and to hear every tongue confess that Jesus Christ is Lord. I really want to see that, and I am praying for it. I sincerely want everyone to know Him and to experience His radiant glory which brings even greater glory to Father God. I want everyone to know Him for their own salvation, and for their part of the great harvest of souls to bring Him the honor and glory He so richly desires. How about you? What are you praying for right now? May it bring glory to both Jesus Christ and Father God! Amen!

The Word teaches that when people see Jesus they see the Father.

"Jesus said to him, 'Have I been with you so long, and yet you have not known Me, Philip? He who has seen Me has seen the Father; so how can you say, '"Show us the Father'"? Do you not believe that I am in the Father, and the Father in Me?'" (John 14:9-10a)

Considering this clear teaching by Jesus and the entire Word of God, I ask you to reflect on the following question. When people who are not believers see you, do they see Jesus? Do they see the light of His glory? If and when they are able to see the light of His glory in you, do they then see the light of the glory of Father God? Some people quickly tell me that they are not like Jesus and cannot do what He did. If you are feeling that way right now, read aloud and meditate on the passage below. Remember that Biblical meditation is repeating something over and over in order to fully grasp and believe it.

"Most assuredly, I say to you, he who believes in Me, the works that I do he will do also; and greater works than these he will do, because I go to My Father. And whatever you ask in My name, that I will do, that the Father may be glorified in the Son. If you ask anything in My name, I will do it." (John 14:12-14)

Every time I use this verse, I ask people if they believe what Jesus said. People always say that they do believe Jesus said this. Did you notice that this response does not really answer the question? It may well be true, but it is not what I asked. This is the essence of the problem. People believe that Jesus said this, but they don't really believe it is true. They do not believe that they can do the things Jesus did and they certainly don't believe that they can do more than He did. This brings up another problem. How can we be disciples of Jesus if we don't believe that what He says is the truth? Do these people believe that Jesus was a liar? If they think this way, how can they serve Him?

If you believe that what Jesus said was the truth, are you living up to it? Are you doing what He did? Are you doing more than He did? My heart desire is to be able to live up to the commands of Jesus and to be able to do whatever He commands me to do. How about you? Think about it: If you started doing greater things than Jesus did, would that bring glory to Him and to Father God? It most certainly will result in glory to God. If you are doing the things He did, people will begin to see Him when they look at you.

Here is another key concept: Your obedience brings glory to the Father.

EFFECTIVE PRAYER WILL BRING THE GLORY OF GOD

Prayers which are based on unity and agreement bring the power of God to bear on our situation and into our ministry. When the power of God is released and prayers are wondrously and powerfully answered, it always brings glory to our Father God. Now, let's take it a step further and bring it up another notch. When God is glorified, He will manifest His glory presence. This is another level of the issue. We're not just talking about bringing the kind of glory to Him that will result in people giving Him praise and thanksgiving. We are talking about bringing Him in all His Glory into our presence on the earth! We can literally experience the answer to our prayers for His kingdom to come on Earth as it is in Heaven.

"And it came to pass when the priests came out of the Most Holy Place (for all the priests who were present had sanctified themselves, without keeping to their divi-

sions), and the Levites who were the singers, all those of Asaph and Heman and Jeduthun, with their sons and their brethren, stood at the east end of the altar, clothed in white linen, having cymbals, stringed instruments and harps, and with them one hundred and twenty priests sounding with trumpets—indeed it came to pass, when the trumpeters and singers were as one, to make one sound to be heard in praising and thanking the Lord, and when they lifted up their voice with the trumpets and cymbals and instruments of music, and praised the Lord, saying: "For He is good, For His mercy endures forever," that the house, the house of the Lord, was filled with a cloud, so that the priests could not continue ministering because of the cloud; for the glory of the Lord filled the house of God." (2 Chronicles 5:11-14)

Imagine this scene: 120 priests blowing shofars (with many different tones), many loud clashing cymbals, stringed instruments of all types (each with their own unique sounds and tones), and a large number of professional quality singers all joining together to praise the Lord. When I first read this, it sounded like the formula for chaos. However the scriptures tell us something so amazing about this event that it is difficult for us to fully grasp it. All of these joined together to make *"one sound."* How is that possible? I believe that this passage is speaking about a level of spiritual unity and agreement which we seldom see in our world today. As one, in total unity, they lifted their praise to the Lord, and He responded in an awesome way.

He did something spectacular which they had never personally seen. Many may have heard about it when the stories were told of the children of Israel being led through the wilderness to the Promised Land. The cloud of His presence came down on the temple as it had in the days of Moses and Joshua. They could see it! They could feel it! The God of Israel descended once again to dwell with His people. That was and still is amazing! It is awesome! I want to see that! I have been earnestly, fervently praying for it for a very long time. Perhaps we will one day achieve the kind of unity that will bring His Glory down like this again. Think about it: they made one sound, and the glory came down! Are you longing for this? I am both hungry and thirsty for His presence and I am living in expectancy that it will come again. Amen and Amen!

They didn't really do anything spectacular. They didn't have some great new praise song that opened heaven. They didn't have personal righteousness which would lead us to say it was because of them. They didn't do some great work which pleased God. They did something so simple we can almost miss it. In unity they sang this repetitious verse: *"For He is good, For His mercy endures forever,"*

That's it! That's all they did, and God appeared. I have tried this in some churches who were seeking His glory presence, and it still works. To understand this, you must see the key ingredients. It has to be done in complete unity as if making only one sound. It must be done in sincerity and love. It must be done in simplicity, recognizing that it is not about us but about Him. It is in His very nature to manifest Himself to those who seek Him in Spirit and in truth. Perhaps the psalmist was thinking about this when He wrote:

> *"Oh, give thanks to the Lord, for He is good! For His mercy endures forever. Let Israel now say, "His mercy endures forever."* (Psalm 118:1-2)

Humility in prayer brings the glory of the Lord. Parts of this psalm are sung as the last song in the Passover Seder. Matthew tells us in the twenty sixth chapter of his gospel that after the meal, they sang a song before going to the Mount of Olives. It would have been this song which points to the stone the builders rejected which then became the chief cornerstone.

Simplicity and humility touch the heart of God. When we add these attitudes of the heart to the unity of our spirits, we invoke the presence of the Lord.

"So Moses and Aaron went from the presence of the assembly to the door of the tabernacle of meeting, and they fell on their faces. And the glory of the Lord appeared to them." (Numbers 20:6)

Moses was always willing to have face time with the Lord, and it is clear the Lord liked to spend time with him. In the stories about Moses in the Bible, we see him over and over face down before the Lord. Consider the response of the Lord to this humble attitude. The Lord spoke with him face to face.

"Then He said, 'Hear now My words: If there is a prophet among you, I, the Lord, make Myself known to him in a vision; I speak to him in a dream. Not so with My servant Moses; He is faithful in all My house. I speak with him face to face, Even plainly, and not in dark sayings; And he sees the form of the Lord. Why then were you not afraid to speak against My servant Moses?'" (Numbers 12:6-8)

Living in a right relationship with the Lord brings Him glory. When we bring Him glory, He responds by sharing His glory with us.

"Also your people shall all be righteous; They shall inherit the land forever, The branch of My planting, The work of My hands, That I may be glorified." (Isaiah 60:21)

Here is an important truth: The Lord can't really meet with unrighteous people. Over and over we read in the scriptures that people honestly believed that when sinful people meet God face to face they will surely die. So, you may ask, "How then can we ever see Him or experience His Glory Presence? The children of Israel clung to this fear and missed their opportunity to meet with Him face to face. But, you don't need to worry! You have received the righteousness of Christ. *"For He made Him who knew no sin to be sin for us, that we might become the righteousness of God in Him."* (2 Corinthians 5:21)

The glory of God has wonderful side effects. Look again at Isaiah 60 and note all the benefits which come to those upon whom the light of God shines.

> *"Arise, shine; For your light has come! And the glory of the Lord is risen upon you. For behold, the darkness shall cover the earth, And deep darkness the people; But the Lord will arise over you, And <u>His glory will be seen</u> upon you. The Gentiles shall come to your light, And kings to the brightness of your rising. "Lift up your eyes all around, and see: They all gather together, they come to you; Your sons shall come from afar, And your daughters shall be nursed at your side. Then you shall see and become radiant, And your heart shall swell with joy; Because the abundance of the sea shall be turned to you, The wealth of the Gentiles shall come to you."* (Isaiah 60:1-5)

He brings light into your darkness. No matter how deep the darkness around you may seem, God can shine His light into it and come to you in a powerful and awesome display of His glory. As I meditated on this passage, I looked at a closed decorative box on the table in front of me. I knew that there was darkness inside the closed box. As I opened the lid the box was suddenly filled with light. The room in which I was sitting did not turn dark because I opened the box. If we reversed the situation and I was sitting in a dark room and opened a box which had a source of light, the box would not become dark, but the room would instantly be filled with light. It works like this every time. Light always overwhelms, conquers, and replaces darkness. It will happen every time you test it. The light will instantly fill every area in the dark place. When God shines His light into your dark place, it will be completely filled with His glory.

This passage also tells us that the Lord restores relationships. It is amazing to consider all that the Glory of God can accomplish without any effort on our part. Isaiah proclaims that unbelievers, rulers, sons, and daughters will return to you when the Glory manifests. I love this passage. I want all my relationships to be healed and restored. When you experience His glory, it just happens by His power and His work. I am so thankful that He has this ministry of reconciliation. With this wonderful news comes a challenge. You have also been called into this ministry of reconciliation. Don't worry about it! Just accept it! He does all the heavy lifting and you get all the benefits.

I believe that we all like the idea of the wealth of the nations coming to the righteous. But we are not always sure how that works. Again, it comes when the Glory of God appears. The only thing the Lord requires on our part is to be willing to work with Him. Too many people resist this work of the Lord. They want people to humble themselves and beg for forgiveness rather than just coming back and expecting things to be okay. I just have one thing to say: Get over it! Well, maybe I have two things to say. The second one is: Get over yourself! God doesn't think like we think or act the way we act. It is not His task to change and be more like us. It is our task to change and be more like Him. How does He plan to do it? When His glory manifests, all will be drawn to Him and then drawn to one another. When this happens, it will bring great glory and praise to Him.

EVERYTHING WE DO SHOULD BRING GLORY TO GOD

"Therefore, whether you eat or drink, or whatever you do, do all to the glory of God." (1 Corinthians 10:31)

Have you ever meditated on this passage? When I thought about it and spoke it over and over I noticed that it became more amazing and more real each time. Can you think of any ways you can eat which will bring glory to God? I immediately thought about hosting a dinner for the homeless and sitting down to eat with them. As I share with them that the Lord made this happen, it would bring Him glory. When we go out to eat, we always pray before the meal. Perhaps someone will see and give glory to God. If our small acts of obedience bring Him glory, how much more should our prayers bring glory to God?

"Give to the Lord, O families of the peoples, Give to the Lord glory and strength. Give to the Lord the glory due His name; Bring an offering, and come into His courts." (Psalm 96:7-8)

I was taught that we do this when we sing and praise Him. That is true to a certain extent, but it doesn't go far enough! We need to intentionally give Him glory in our prayers. We need to stay focused on what we pray; making sure that what we ask will bring Him glory from others. Think about this. How will you manage to do this? Offerings and prayers of thanks are good, but they don't go far enough by themselves. I believe that something more is meant by this and it is our task to discover what it is and put it into practice. Then I noticed that last little phrase *"and come into His courts."* How much time are you spending in His courts? I believe this is the key. He wants us! He wants us more than the songs, the offering, and

206

the prayers. He wants us to come back to Him. So much is said here about restoring relationships and the most important of all is our relationship with Father God. Get ready and come into His courts often!

Examine yourself! Do your prayers focus on bringing Him glory? If you find that the things you are praying for will not actually bring Him glory, you need to change what you are seeking. If you don't bring glory to Him, it will come anyway, but you will not reap the harvest from it.

> "And some of the Pharisees called to Him from the crowd, 'Teacher, rebuke Your disciples.' But He answered and said to them, 'I tell you that if these should keep silent, the stones would immediately cry out.'" (Luke 19:39-40)

These words seem a little harsh at first. How does it feel to know that you can be replaced by a common old stone? Just remember that God will be glorified one way or another. The difference is in who will be blessed by it. If you don't bring glory to God, it will come anyway, but tragically, you will miss the blessing.

I pray that the Lord will break off everything that hinders you! I pray that He will release an anointing for you to move to a higher level as an intercessor warrior. I pray that you will move up into the glory zone with Him! I pray that He will move so powerfully in your life and ministry that everything you do will bring more and more glory to Him! Amen!

Here is another important truth which many people have great difficulty in receiving and manifesting. You cannot really pray this way if you are filled with bitterness and un-forgiveness. God will not answer prayers founded on something so distasteful to Him. Consider again what Jesus said about the subject of forgiveness.

"For if you forgive men their trespasses, your heavenly Father will also forgive you. But if you do not forgive men their trespasses, neither will your Father forgive your trespasses." (Matthew 6:14-15)

This is the point at which so many people become totally blocked. They just can't let go of past hurts. They cannot find it in their hearts to forgive people who have hurt them, offended them, or embarrassed them. Sometimes people are holding onto hurts which go back many years. Often the person or persons from whom they are withholding forgiveness are not even aware of the problem. Some unforgiving people are still losing sleep, having difficulty eating and nursing ulcers over things which the other party has long forgotten. The object of their anger is unaffected, but they are imprisoned by their own hate filled thoughts and feelings. In effect, they have blocked themselves to the flow of blessing in their own lives. Forgiveness will set them free to be blessed and to have a glorious relationship with the Lord. Now think about it for a minute. Have you ever met a person filled with anger, hatred, and un-forgiveness whose behavior inspired you to think about how much their behavior was bringing glory to God? Of course not! It just doesn't work that way. Whatever old hurt or offense you may be holding on to, let it go and get back into the Glory of God.

Here is another powerful truth: When you bring Him glory, He hears your prayers, releases an outpouring of glory, blessing, and favor, and establishes a wall of protection around you.

"Then your light shall break forth like the morning, Your healing shall spring forth speedily, And your righteousness shall go before you; The glory of the Lord shall be your rear guard. Then you shall call, and the Lord will answer; You shall cry, and He will say, 'Here I am.'" (Isaiah 58:8-9a)

Isn't this what you truly want for yourself and those you lift up in your intercessory prayers? Think about the benefits coming to you and to them:

1. *"The glory of the Lord shall be your rear guard."*
2. *"Then you shall call, and the Lord will answer;*
3. *You shall cry, and He will say, 'Here I am.'"*

Giving glory to God brings some powerful and amazing things to you. You will invoke Him and His fire and power. As a retired military officer, I like firepower. How about you? Do you want and need some more fire and power in your life and ministry? If you want these things, give Him glory for everything. If you want more of His presence and power in your life and ministry, then do the things which bring Him glory. He always blesses these behaviors. He always comes to those who faithfully obey Him and give all the glory to Him.

"When Solomon had finished praying, fire came down from heaven and consumed the burnt offering and the sacrifices; and the glory of the Lord filled the temple. And the priests could not enter the house of the Lord, because the glory of the Lord had filled the Lord's house. When all the children of Israel saw how the fire came down, and the glory of the Lord on the temple, they bowed their faces to the ground on the pavement, and worshiped and praised the Lord, saying: "For He is good, For His mercy endures forever." (2 Chronicles 7:1-3)

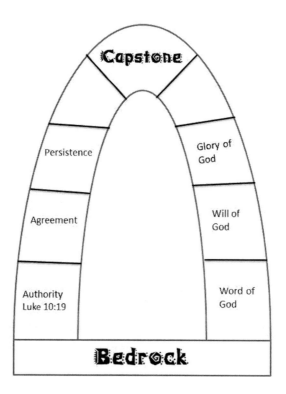

Glory of God: The Sixth Stone in the Foundation

CHAPTER 7

THE STONE OF POSITIONING

❧❧

When the Lord revealed this stone, my mind was flooded with so many ideas about what this could mean. There are many teachings today which focus on how to properly position yourself for success. These teachings have immerged in the secular realm at the same time as they have been released in church settings. As I thought about these simultaneous moves from the secular and sacred communities to understand positioning, I was inspired to look up the definition of positioning in several dictionaries. I was surprised to see that these concepts apply to all seven mountains of culture. The challenge was no longer what to include for this chapter, but what to exclude to stay focused on the revelation of the Lord.

I narrowed the topic down to the following areas or types of positions:

1. Positioning geographically in the place of your anointing.
2. Positioning occupationally in order to support your calling
3. Positioning in a ministry which matches your anointing.
4. Positioning theologically as an intercessor warrior.
5. Positioning on the foundation stones given by the Lord.

POSITIONING IN THE PLACE
OF YOUR ANOINTING

*"You did not choose me, but I chose you and appointed
you to go and bear fruit—fruit that will last. Then the
Father will give you whatever you ask in my name."*
(John 15:16, NIV)

You must always remember that it is the Lord who chooses
you and the position of your anointing. When the Lord gives
you an anointing it is not a reward for good behavior or to
confer a title which will bring respect to you. He calls, anoints,
and positions to meet a specific need in a specific location. Are
you currently in the location of your anointing? Many people
are just not in the right place at the right time. When you follow
the leadership of the Holy Spirit, He will get you to the right
place at the right time and bless your ministry with increase
and abundant fruit.

If you are not seeing very much fruit in your ministry right
now, it is a good time to ask the Lord if you are in the right
place at the right time. When you make this request, you need
to be ready and willing to relocate according to His command
and in accordance with the anointing He has given to you.

As the Lord began to reveal this message about "foundation
stones" to us a few years ago, one of the first things He did was
tell us to relocate. When the Lord said, "Move," He didn't say
where, when or how. Has this happened to you? I don't know
what you would do, but I know that my wife and I started to
get our house ready to sell. As we stepped out in this prophetic
word, the Lord gradually revealed where and when. Then He
provided the how. In a poor housing market, our house sold for
much more than we had paid for it. This made it possible for us
to pay the moving costs, and to get the house which the Lord
had chosen for us in the new location.

People from the area where we were previously located had difficulty understanding or accepting our choice to move to a new location without knowing anyone there or having a job waiting for us. People in our new location were equally challenged in accepting our choice. The truth is that we were not moving according to their plan or understanding. We moved because the Lord told us to relocate to a new geographical area. When we obeyed, the Lord opened up the floodgates of Heaven and poured out so many blessings on us and our new ministry that we have had difficulty containing all of it.

The Lord called us to move to the city were Interstate Highway I-77 begins and to intercede for a move of God along the corridor created by that road. People in the new location resented it when we shared with them how God had called us to this place to intercede over the area. They thought we were accusing them of doing an inadequate job in prayer. This was not our purpose or a part of the command of the Lord, He sent us to provide additional support for their work through daily intercession. This did not appease them. They had taken offense at our anointing and had no intention of letting their anger go. I am sharing these experiences for a reason. Don't expect people to bless your choices when you relocate to the place of the Lord's calling and your anointing. Do it for the Lord! Do it for Him alone, and He will bless it!

Too many intercessors have tried to position themselves in the place of their choosing rather than following the Lord's plan. The results have not always been good for them or those under their ministry. When you call yourself to a ministry without listening to the Lord you may get the results of the seven sons of Sceva.

"Then some of the itinerant Jewish exorcists took it upon themselves to call the name of the Lord Jesus over those who had evil spirits, saying, "We exorcise you by the Jesus whom Paul preaches." Also there were seven

sons of Sceva, a Jewish chief priest, who did so. And the evil spirit answered and said, "Jesus I know, and Paul I know; but who are you?" Then the man in whom the evil spirit was leaped on them, overpowered them, and prevailed against them, so that they fled out of that house naked and wounded. This became known both to all Jews and Greeks dwelling in Ephesus; and fear fell on them all, and the name of the Lord Jesus was magnified." (Acts 19:13-17)

I want the name of Jesus to be magnified, but not in this way. Can you imagine the stories which went around after this fiasco? Before you go to battle with the enemy as an intercessor warrior, you want to be certain that you have an anointing to do that at this time and in this place. When you operate in your anointing and the authority and power the Lord gives, the demons will know your name. Some people don't want the enemy to know their names. If that is your attitude, you may need to step down from your position as an intercessor. You may need to break free from a spirit of fear and realize that the enemy always knows the names of the Lord's anointed ones.

When the enemy knows your name, he knows your authority and the power of God which goes with it. You don't do it in the name someone else proclaims. You do it in the mighty name of Jesus whom you serve. Keep going back to Luke 10:19 and speaking your authority over the power of the enemy. Go back over James 4:7 to understand what you need to do to cause him to flee. Then you will be able to magnify the name of Jesus and bring glory to Father God through your ministry and intercessory prayers.

"So the Lord has fulfilled His word which He spoke; and I have filled <u>the position</u> of my father David, and sit on the throne of Israel, as the Lord promised; and I have

built a temple for the name of the Lord God of Israel."
(1 Kings 8:20)

Solomon had a clear understanding of how he became King of Israel. It was not by his choice, capabilities, talent, charisma, or family position. He had been chosen by God and would only be able to maintain the position by the will and with the help of the Lord. According to his writings, Solomon understood that the Lord had chosen him before he was prepared to step into the position. During the time between the prophesy and the manifestation, the Lord blessed him with the wisdom and understanding necessary to succeed as king.

Like Solomon, you must learn to position yourself where the Lord tells you to stand. Are you in that place right now? Are you experiencing victory and seeing much fruit from your labors? If not, ask the Lord for wisdom and understanding so that you can accomplish His purpose for your life. I love the story of the victory the Lord gave during the time Jehoshaphat was king.

> *"You will not need to fight in this battle. <u>Position your-selves</u>, stand still and see the salvation of the Lord, who is with you, O Judah and Jerusalem!' Do not fear or be dismayed; tomorrow go out against them, for the Lord is with you." And Jehoshaphat bowed his head with his face to the ground, and all Judah and the inhabitants of Jerusalem bowed before the Lord, worshiping the Lord."* (2 Chronicles 20:17-18)

Notice that in this passage of scripture that the Lord had established a position for Jehoshaphat. To activate the prophecy and get the results promised by the Lord, he had to get moving and get to that location. Notice what the Lord said to him, *"<u>Position yourselves</u>."* It is the Lord's doing. It is His will, but you have to position yourself where and when He tells you in order to get the results you seek. That is where we see something amazing! When Jehoshaphat obeyed the Lord he received a God-sized outcome. When he arrived, the victory had already been won.

> *"So when Judah came to a place overlooking the wilderness, they looked toward the multitude; and there were their dead bodies, fallen on the earth. No one had escaped. When Jehoshaphat and his people came to take away their spoil, they found among them an abundance of valuables on the dead bodies, and precious jewelry, which they stripped off for themselves, more than they could carry away; and they were three days gathering the spoil because there was so much."* (2 Chronicles 20:24-25)

Wouldn't you like to fight all your battles this way? Just go to the position the Lord decrees and watch Him work. Jehoshaphat and his people went from poverty to prosperity in one day. They went from threatened disaster to a total victory by simply getting into their assigned position. Because they turned to the Lord in humility and only asked His help to provide for their basic survival needs, He gave them abundantly above and beyond what they asked or imagined. It took them three days to pick up all the treasure left behind by their enemies. The wealth of the wicked had been powerfully transferred to the righteous. When they gave God the praise and the glory for this awesome victory, the Lord established a lengthy time of rest for them.

> *"So they came to Jerusalem, with stringed instruments and harps and trumpets, to the house of the Lord. And the fear of God was on all the kingdoms of those countries when they heard that the Lord had fought against the enemies of Israel. Then the realm of Jehoshaphat*

was quiet, for his God gave him rest all around." (2 Chronicles 20:28-30)

The awesome power of God was released when His obedient people allowed Him to position them in the place of their anointing. He blessed the people with victory, prosperity, peace, quiet, and rest. Some people seem to be in spiritual warfare all the time. They keep on entering into one battle after another until they become unable to function from the stress, fatigue, and wounds of their warfare. This is not the Lord's way. The Lord wants you to have times of rest, relaxation, refreshing and renewal. He wants to fight most of your battles for you. He wants you to wait in obedience for His call and move into position when He tells you to move. The rewards for obedience are wonderful and amazing!

You need to understand that just as the Lord puts his servants into a position, He can also remove people from their position. Even those who have had great victories in the past can become disobedient and unwilling to follow the Lord's most recent commands. When that happens, the Lord will make every attempt to restore His servants to their place of anointing. If all His attempts fail because people are unwilling to obey, He may decide to remove them from their office of ministry. It has happened many times in the past and it will happen again in the future. The Lord sent a message through the prophet Isaiah to Shebna who was a steward over the house of David in Judah.

"So I will drive you out of your office, and from your position he will pull you down." (Isaiah 22:19)

The Word of God clearly teaches that you can be removed from your position. I have heard many manmade doctrines which say this cannot happen. These so called doctrines actually come from false teaching. Always go to the Word of God rather than the word of man. If there is a conflict of opinion, the Word is correct every time. Peter was a graduate of the Lord's school of ministry. He was under the personal teaching and mentoring of Jesus for three years. Consider what Peter taught on this subject of falling from your position.

> *"Therefore, dear friends, since you already know this, be on your guard so that you may not be carried away by the error of lawless men and <u>fall from your secure position</u>. But grow in the grace and knowledge of our Lord and Savior Jesus Christ. To him be glory both now and forever! Amen."* (2 Peter 3:17-18, NIV)

The Bible says that it is okay to desire a position of service in the kingdom of God. When you think about requesting a specific position, consider carefully what you are seeking. If you desire to be positioned in a place of anointing by the Lord you must be ready to meet His standards.

> *"This is a faithful saying: If a man desires the position of a bishop, he desires a good work. A bishop then must be blameless, the husband of one wife, temperate, sober-minded, of good behavior, hospitable, able to teach; not given to wine, not violent, not greedy for money, but gentle, not quarrelsome, not covetous; one who rules his own house well, having his children in submission with all reverence (for if a man does not know how to rule his own house, how will he take care of the church of God?); not a novice, lest being puffed up with pride he fall into the same condemnation as the devil. Moreover he must have a good testimony among those who are outside, lest he fall into reproach and the snare of the devil."* (1 Timothy 3:1-7)

Remember that the Lord didn't call you because you are talented, smart, pretty or because you are a one of a kind invaluable servant. It was by grace and by grace alone that you were allowed to move into a position and anointing of the Lord. It is His work and His plan. If you faithfully obey and follow His leadership, you will remain secure in your position. We should be humbled by the Lord's choice to put us into a place of anointing and remain humble while in the office. Remember that the Lord elevates the humble and brings down the proud.

> *"The brother in humble circumstances ought to take pride in his high position. But the one who is rich should take pride in his low position, because he will pass away like a wild flower. For the sun rises with scorching heat and withers the plant; its blossom falls and its beauty is destroyed. In the same way, the rich man will fade away even while he goes about his business."* (James 1:9-11, NIV)

POSITIONING OCCUPATIONALLY TO SUPPORT YOUR CALLING

Some people are called to positions of full time ministry with a salary which provides adequate income to support them and their families. Others are called to part time positions which do not pay enough for their full support. In this case, they need to have another paying job in addition to their ministry. Still others are in a ministry with no salary and have to have all their income from another source. All of these situations are okay if they are the calling of the Lord. Many who have been called to work in both secular and ministry settings actually provide ministry in both positions. If the Lord calls, He will provide.

Speaking about people in an itinerant ministry, Jesus said *"the laborer is worthy of his wages."* (Luke 10:7b) Paul combined this word from the Lord with Deuteronomy 25:4 which says, *"You shall not muzzle an ox while it treads out the grain."* Then he advised his spiritual son Timothy to put this concept into practice in his ministry.

> *"For the Scripture says, 'You shall not muzzle an ox while it treads out the grain,' and, 'The laborer is worthy of his wages.'"* (1 Timothy 5:18)

I'm not sure how many people in ministry want to be called an "ox," but the point is well made. A person who uses a beast of burden to do his work will not starve the animal to the point that it cannot do the work. In the same way, we should not expect people to labor in ministry without pay.

How does this apply to the intercessors? With a few exceptions in the corporate world where intercessors have been known to be in salaried positions, most intercessors are in unpaid positions. As volunteers, they must have another source of income for their livelihood. If you must do that, it is very important to have an occupation which is compatible with and supportive of your ministry commitment. This does not always happen in the corporate world.

It is good for the members of an intercessory group to pray for one another in agreement and in accordance with the Word of God for people on their prayer teams to find occupations which are compatible with their ministry. It is also appropriate to seek help from the Lord to find a job which will enhance rather than distract from you commitment to Him and to your service in the kingdom.

The enemy can use work place issues to distract you from your focus on the Lord. As an intercessor, you are being built up into a spiritual house, and you need to keep the house of the Lord clean and pure.

> *"As you come to him, the living Stone—rejected by men but chosen by God and precious to him—you also, like*

living stones, are being built into a spiritual house to be a holy priesthood, offering spiritual sacrifices acceptable to God through Jesus Christ." (1 Peter 2:4-5, NIV)

POSITIONING IN A MINISTRY MATCHING YOUR ANOINTING

"He who descended is the very one who ascended higher than all the heavens, in order to fill the whole universe. It was he who gave some to be apostles, some to be prophets, some to be evangelists, and some to be pastors and teachers, to prepare God's people for works of service, so that the body of Christ may be built up until we all reach unity in the faith and in the knowledge of the Son of God and become mature, attaining to the whole measure of the fullness of Christ." (Ephesians 4:10-13, NIV)

Many people are in ministry positions which are not actually compatible with their calling. Not all pastors are called at an early age to be senior pastors. Yet, many aspire to the position for personal reasons. Some of them have a strong need or desire for greater status, influence, or personal satisfaction. Personal needs, feelings, and aspirations are not adequate foundations for a position and they do not make up for the lack of anointing for the position. Some people with a rebellious spirit are simply unwilling to follow the leadership of another person. To avoid the issues, they may seek to replace the person who is supervising them. This can result in the kind of disaster people used to refer to as a "train wreck" of the souls of those involved.

Remember the situation (described in the book of Numbers, chapter sixteen) when Korah, Dathan, Abiram, and On decided to step into Moses' anointing. They led a rebellion against God's chosen and anointed leaders to meet their own personal needs. This rebellion eventually resulted in the tragic deaths of over fifteen thousand people. I want to give you two general rules concerning positioning yourself in the Lord's anointing.

1. You are at your best when you are functioning in the area of your anointing!

2. You are at your worst when you try to step into someone else's anointing!

There may be exceptions to this rule, but I have never personally seen one. Without the anointing of the Lord you cannot succeed for very long. You can only get so far on your own skills, abilities, and personality. Eventually it will catch up to you. Without the blessing and favor of the Lord, you will not be able to lead people very far.

Even with blessing and favor, Moses found it difficult to lead the people. Consider this: Even the Lord Jesus experienced rebellion, betrayal, and abandonment from those who agreed to follow Him. Do you actually believe that you will be able to handle it better than Jesus and Moses?

In a rebellion, there is only one place to go. There is only one person you can turn to for wisdom, guidance and support. You have to take it to the Lord. If you are not in alignment with His calling and anointing, you are going to have a very difficult time resolving your leadership problems.

What is your calling? Can you clearly affirm that it was the Lord who called you and anointed you for the position you are in right now? I have met so many people in ministry who were called by their parents, pastor, or teachers. They initially thought that was enough, but when hard times came, they tended to fall away. I have met many intercessors who were called by other members of a prayer team rather than by the Lord. The members of the prayer team thought they needed more people and took it upon themselves to select and call people to the positions. This is another recipe for disaster and a "shipwreck" of the souls involved. I am convinced that the only intercessors that are successful and effective over the long-haul have been called by God and given a definite anointing for the position.

POSITIONING THEOLOGICALLY AS AN INTERCESSOR WARRIOR

A calling to the position of intercessor is a high calling. Intercessors are often the unsung heroes in the background doing warfare so that the ministry of others can go forward in the blessing and favor of the Lord. Most of the people being blessed and protected through their fervent and continuous prayers are often unaware of their existence much less their support. These intercessor warriors keep doing what they are doing because they are committed to the Lord and to the building up of His kingdom.

The highest office of intercession is occupied by the Lord Jesus. The writer of Hebrews reminds us of someone behind the scenes who is constantly praying on our behalf. I don't know about you, but I am greatly encouraged to know that Jesus is interceding for me. The writer of Hebrews says:

"Because of this oath, Jesus has become the guarantee of a better covenant. Now there have been many of those priests, since death prevented them from continuing in office; but because Jesus lives forever, he has a permanent priesthood. Therefore he is able to save completely those who come to God through him, because he always lives to intercede for them." (Hebrews 7:22-25, NIV)

Paul confirmed this message about the Lord Jesus being our intercessor in his letter to the church at Rome. Jesus has a position given by Father God and He is in His assigned position. He is obediently serving to support us by sitting at the right hand of God so that He can intercede on our behalf. This is such an awesome thought. When we accept a calling as an intercessor warrior, we are put in our position on a team and at the same time with the Lord as head of the team in His position. What a team!

> "Who *is* he who condemns? *It is* Christ who died, and furthermore is also risen, who is even at the right hand of God, who also makes intercession for us." (Romans 8:34)

That would be enough, but it gets better. We have a double portion blessing in everything because the Lord has sent the Holy Spirit to support and guide us. In addition to all His other duties, He is also an intercessor on our behalf.

> *"Likewise the Spirit also helps in our weaknesses. For we do not know what we should pray for as we ought, but the Spirit Himself makes intercession for us with groanings which cannot be uttered. Now He who searches the hearts knows what the mind of the Spirit is, because He makes intercession for the saints according to the will of God."* (Romans 8:26-27)

The Holy Spirit is in His position as assigned by the Father. He is in your heart where He can know everything about you. He knows more about you than you know about yourself. He prays through you with insight and power you cannot understand. All you may hear is a deep groaning coming from within you but which is not from you. It is the Holy Spirit interceding for you according to the will of God.

These are awesome thoughts that are almost too wonderful for us to grasp and accept. Father God has thought of everything to make sure we succeed and are enabled to function in our positions with His blessing and favor. Awesome!

One more thing must be said. All of this is activated by your faith. With all of the mighty and wonderful things provided by Father God, Jesus Christ and the Holy Spirit, you must still add your personal faith in order to bring God's power to your situation.

> *"Jesus replied, 'I tell you the truth, if you have faith and do not doubt, not only can you do what was done to the fig tree, but also you can say to this mountain, 'Go, throw yourself into the sea,' and it will be done. If you believe, you will receive whatever you ask for in prayer."* (Matthew 21:21-22, ((NIV)

POSITIONING ON THE LORD'S FOUNDATION STONES

Once occupied, your position needs to be strengthened if you are going to be able to stand against enemy attacks. This strengthening of positions is mentioned over and over in the Bible. It is mentioned most often related to the position of a king or some other established leadership position. Some people got off to a shaky start because of an untimely elevation to their position. Some got started on a very weak foundation as the government or nation was being brought down by the Lord. Others started on a solid foundation, but still had to establish their right to be in the position by strengthening it. If you are blessed to begin on a strong foundation, your task will be easier and lighter, but you still have to establish yourself there.

> *"Afterward, the prophet came to the king of Israel and said, 'Strengthen your position and see what must be done, because next spring the king of Aram will attack you again.'"* (1 Kings 20:22, NIV)

The good news for intercessors is that Father God has called you to take your stand on a sure foundation which He

Himself has built. This foundation will endure forever. The Apostle Paul considered himself to be an *"expert builder ["By the grace God has given me, I laid a foundation as an expert builder, and someone else is building on it."* (1 Corinthians 3:10, NIV)] What could make Paul feel so confident about the foundation he had built for the church in Corinth? He build on the solid rock of the Lord Jesus. The good news is that the foundation is already in place and your task is to wisely build on it.

> *"But each one should be careful how he builds. For no one can lay any foundation other than the one already laid, which is Jesus Christ. If any man builds on this foundation using gold, silver, costly stones, wood, hay or straw, his work will be shown for what it is, because the Day will bring it to light. It will be revealed with fire, and the fire will test the quality of each man's work. If what he has built survives, he will receive his reward. If it is burned up, he will suffer loss; he himself will be saved, but only as one escaping through the flames. Don't you know that you yourselves are God's temple and that God's Spirit lives in you? If anyone destroys God's temple, God will destroy him; for God's temple is sacred, and you are that temple."* (1 Corinthians 3:11-7, NIV)

Now it is your turn to build on the foundation. You must wisely choose the correct materials you will use for building. Will you use gold, silver, and precious stones or will you build with hay and straw? As you build be aware that a time of testing is coming. Everything you build will be tested in the fire of God's righteous judgment. Please notice how critical your building is. You are building yourself up into that dwelling place for the Lord. You are the Temple of God and it is a house which must be sacred to Him. Be very certain that you are building on the precious cornerstone!

It is much better to examine yourself now and make adjustments to get back into the correct position than to wait for the judgment of the Lord. Reflecting on the foundation stones we have covered up to this point, begin to ask yourself where you are standing. Are you positioned firmly on these stones? Or, have you gotten off the foundation stones of the Lord? It is your task to keep yourself in the position the Lord has established for your ministry. It is your responsibility and the Lord will hold you accountable.

Are you firmly anchored on the stone of authority? Does the authority given with your position show in your everyday life, your prayers, and your ministry? Do you pray with authority? Many people affirm that Jesus was telling the truth in Luke 10:19, *"Behold, I give you the authority to trample on serpents and scorpions, and over all the power of the enemy, and nothing shall by any means hurt you."* Yet it is difficult to hear an authoritative voice when they pray. We have had enough of the wimpy and wishy-washy prayers. It is time to stand in faith firmly planted on the stone of authority and make powerful kingdom decrees in your prayers.Do you have one foot firmly planted on the stone of God's Word? Examine yourself using the teaching in Hebrews 5:12, *"In fact, though by this time you ought to be teachers, you need someone to teach you the elementary truths of God's word all over again. You need milk, not solid food!"* Have you moved from the milk of the Word to the meat of the Word? Are you positioned on the Word of God with a stance which makes you unmovable? Remember that this is how Jesus dealt with the enemy and it will work for you. Spend as much time as possible in the Word of God reading it aloud so that it becomes yours and for it to build you up in the power of faith. Literally, standing on the Word of God, positions you on the foundation stone of faith.

Have you taken your stand on the stone of agreement? Jesus gives us an assurance that whatever we ask in agreement we will receive. It is important to be in agreement with other believers. However, it is more important for you to be in agreement with the Father, the Son, and the Holy Spirit.

"However, when He, the Spirit of truth, has come, He will guide you into all truth; for He will not speak on His own authority, but whatever He hears He will speak; and He will tell you things to come." (John 16:13)

This is how Jesus and the Holy Spirit do their work and you are told to do the same. It is vital to be in agreement with the Word of God. When you line up with all this power and authority, your prayers will be supercharged and produce kingdom results on a consistent basis. Don't let anything push you off this foundation stone!

With each additional stone the foundation is being built up and made stronger. To truly stand firm you need to be standing on the stone which is the will of God. Jesus always stood on this foundation stone. Look again at what He taught about doing the will of the father.

"I can of Myself do nothing. As I hear, I judge; and My judgment is righteous, because I do not seek My own will but the will of the Father who sent Me." (John 5:30)

If doing the will of the Father was that important for Jesus, how much more important is it for you? Are you positioned firmly on the foundation stone of the will of God? Continue to search for Biblical references to the will of God, read the verses aloud, and then memorize them. Be certain that every prayer is not only based on the will of God, but also serves to bring His will to the earth as it is in heaven.

Jesus gave us a model prayer which reinforces this concept. Look again at what Jesus taught in Luke 11:2-4,

"So He said to them, "When you pray, say: Our Father in heaven, Hallowed be Your name. Your kingdom come. ***Your will be done On earth as it is in heaven****. Give us day by day our daily bread. And forgive us our sins, For we also forgive everyone who is indebted to us. And do not lead us into temptation, But deliver us from the evil one."*

As you go higher and higher on the foundation stones you are building your house on a stronger foundation with each stone. It is very important to stand on the stone of persistence. We need to be ready to repel any attempt by the enemy to tempt us to lose faith when things don't happen in our timing. We need to trust more in the timing of the Lord. Study again what Jesus taught in Luke chapter 18. Especially notice the first verse in this chapter, *"Then Jesus told his disciples a parable to show them that they should always pray and not give up."* (NIV) Take your stand and do not give up. Remember the promise in Galatians 6:9, *"And let us not be weary in well doing: for in due season we shall reap, if we faint not."* (KJV). Persistence is a powerful stone. Position yourself firmly on this stone.

Next position yourself firmly on the foundation stone of the glory of God. This seems to be one of the least known foundation stones. This is a two-edged sword. You release great power when you labor and pray to bring glory to God. On the other hand there is a severe penalty for not giving God the glory He is due. Consider what happened to Herod the king when he accepted the glory rather than giving it to God.

"Then immediately an angel of the Lord struck him, because he did not give glory to God. And he was eaten by worms and died." (Acts 12:23)

As you take a firm stance on the stone of God's glory, begin to give Him glory in everything you say and do. Read over again the words of 1 Corinthians 10:31, *"Therefore, whether you eat or drink, or whatever you do, do all to the glory of God."* You can be certain that giving glory to God in everything you do will bring His power to your authority and produce great results for the kingdom of God.

It is important for every believer to be firmly positioned on these foundation stones for prayer. But, if you are an intercessor warrior, taking your stand on these foundation stones is essential. It is the primary place you are to position yourself as you move forward in your service for the Lord! May you always stand firm in your faith and practice!

> *"Be patient, then, brothers, until the Lord's coming. See how the farmer waits for the land to yield its valuable crop and how patient he is for the autumn and spring rains. You too, be patient and stand firm, because the Lord's coming is near. Don't grumble against each other, brothers, or you will be judged. The Judge is standing at the door!"* (James 5:7-9, NIV)

Remember the story of Gideon in the book of Judges. His small group of three hundred men got into their assigned positions according to God's directions. They broke their jars revealing a torch, blew a shofar, shouted, and watched the Lord win a mighty victory. Look closely at what the Bible says they did.

> *"While <u>each man held his position</u> around the camp, all the Midianites ran, crying out as they fled."* (Judges 7:21, NIV)

When you get into the position the Lord has given you and you continue to stand in it, the Lord releases His mighty power to win the battle. True intercessor warriors have learned to get into position and stay in position as they watch the Lord fight the big battles for them.

Are you standing in your assigned position? If not, do everything in your power to get there and stay there!

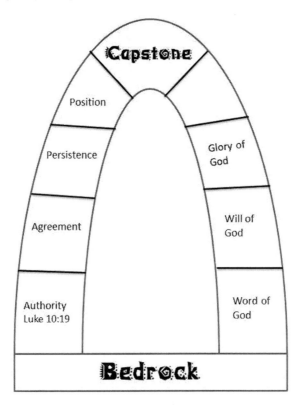

Position: The Seventh Stone in the Foundation

CHAPTER 8

THE STONE OF HIS KINGDOM

⚜ ⚜

*A*s I prepared to write this chapter, I began a new study to help me determine more precisely what the Word of God has to say about the "kingdom of God." I did a search with the Bibles on my computer. In the New King James Version (NKJV), I found sixty nine references to the kingdom of God. All of them were in the New Testament. I expanded the search, and found thirty one references to the kingdom of heaven in the NKJV. All of these references were in the book of Matthew in the New Testament. Matthew was writing specifically to a Jewish audience, and he was sensitive to their beliefs concerning the use of the name of God. Matthew only made reference to the "kingdom of God" five times and each was a direct quote from the Lord Jesus. Because Jesus is the Son of God, He had the kingdom right to speak the name of God. His lips are most certainly pure enough to say "the name." When you are clothed in the righteousness of Jesus, you too can say the name, but you must always speak it in purity and in the fear of the Lord.

Think about it! In the combined Old and New Testaments, prayer is only mentioned one hundred and nine times. While in the New Testament alone, the kingdom of God is mentioned one hundred times. I am convinced that this is an important message for you to receive. I went to my study notes on the Biblical meaning of numbers and found that the number one hundred has three powerful meanings: 1) Maximum Divine Good Production; 2) God's election of grace; and 3) Children of Promise. These are three very powerful aspects of the kingdom of God. These ideas are reinforced by the use of the phrase one hundred times in God's Holy Word. Nothing is in the Word by accident.

I found a reference in the book of Acts which really intrigued me. As you read it aloud, pay close attention to verse three.

"The former account I made, O Theophilus, of all that Jesus began both to do and teach, until the day in which He was taken up, after He through the Holy Spirit had given commandments to the apostles whom He had chosen, to whom He also presented Himself alive after His suffering by many infallible proofs, being seen by them during forty days and <u>speaking of the things pertaining to the kingdom of God</u>." (Acts 1:1-3)

As I read this passage over and over, I developed something of a holy hunger to know what Jesus taught about the kingdom of God during those forty days after His resurrection. Before the resurrection, there were many things He could not teach them because they were not yet ready to understand. After the resurrection, He focused specifically on teaching about the kingdom of God. Jesus had told them that they would not be able to fully understand until they received the Spirit of truth. However, Jesus was teaching them more even though these forty days came before the infilling of the Holy Spirit on the Day of Pentecost. How is this possible? What changed? Then I went to the last chapter of Luke and read the following passage:

"Then He said to them, 'These are the words which I spoke to you while I was still with you, that all things must be fulfilled which were written in the Law of Moses and the Prophets and the Psalms concerning Me.' And He opened their understanding, that they might comprehend the Scriptures." (Luke 24:44-45)

Jesus opened their understanding so that He could complete the teaching He had for them concerning the kingdom of God. When I read this, I got excited. If Jesus did this for them, He can do it for me! So, I prayed: "Lord Jesus open my understanding so that I can comprehend the Scriptures and better understand your teaching about the kingdom of God! Lord Jesus, I pray this to you and to Father God in your Name. Amen!" Then I prayed for you to receive the same gift of wisdom and revelation to help you understand more fully as you read through this chapter.

After praying these intercessory prayers, I felt led to another passage which spoke of Jesus meeting with the disciples during these forty days after the resurrection.

"So Jesus said to them again, 'Peace to you! As the Father has sent Me, I also send you." And when He had said this, He breathed on them, and said to them, "Receive the Holy Spirit.'" (John 20:21-22)

After reading this, I got excited all over again in my spirit. Jesus gave them an early release of the gift of the Holy Spirit by breathing it into them. He gave them the Spirit of truth that day so that He could complete His teaching on the kingdom of God before His ascension. Think about it! If He did it for them, He can do it for you and me.

So, I prayed again, "Lord Jesus, I ask you to breathe on me and release a fresh anointing of the Spirit of truth on me as I seek to understand more about the kingdom of God! I am ready to receive and I am asking both in faith and in agreement with your Word. Now I receive it and give you thanks for it! Amen and Amen!" Next, I prayed this prayer for you.

I encourage you before you go any further to pray this or a similar prayer in order to open up your spirit so that you are able to understand Jesus' lessons about the kingdom of God more completely than you have ever understood them before. I pray that your understanding will be greater than mine, and that you will be enabled to teach, lead, and mentor future disciples to understand these kingdom principles! Amen!

I have a deep desire to know more about the kingdom of God. There seems to be a gap in our knowledge base, because none of the disciples wrote directly about what Jesus taught them. I believe there are at least three things we can do about that. First, study the writings of those who were with him during those forty days and see what they are teaching now that goes beyond what you read in the Gospels. Then, pray the prayers mentioned above for the Lord to teach you. Finally, study what Paul taught because he received his teaching directly from the Lord by revelation knowledge.

I am always seeking more revelation knowledge. How about you? Without the wisdom and understand released by the Spirit of truth combined with the revelation knowledge the Lord gives, you cannot really know what the Lord taught during that forty day period. If you want to know more about the kingdom of God and you are willing to apply yourself to learn and teach these principles, I believe the Lord will answers these prayers and give you more than you have ever asked or imagined.

PRAYING FOR THE KINGDOM OF GOD TO COME

I started out by looking at some of the things we do know. We know these kingdom principles because the Lord taught them and they were recorded in the Bible for us. One thing very clearly taught by Jesus was that we are to pray for the kingdom of God to come on earth.

> *"He said to them, 'When you pray, say: Father, hallowed be your name, **your kingdom come**. Give us each day our daily bread. Forgive us our sins, for we also forgive everyone who sins against us. And lead us not into temptation.'"* (Luke 11:2-4, NIV)

I like to have clarity and understanding about what the Lord wants me to do. I like to have His wisdom and revelation before I begin a task. This is one of those places where we have that clarity. According to Jesus, we absolutely need to pray for His kingdom to come on the earth. When I was growing up, I was taught to pray for His kingdom in heaven. If there was a lesson about the possibility of that kingdom being a reality here while we are still living, I must have slept through the class. Perhaps you had a similar experience with your early Christian Education. Perhaps now is a time to get an understanding with more clarity through the work of the Spirit of truth.

Many people I have met seem to believe that the only thing Jesus was asking for us to do was to tack the phrase "your kingdom come" on the end of long prayers for other things. I am convinced that Jesus meant much more than this. He taught many things about what the kingdom was to be like and we are responsible for getting the pearls of wisdom from these teachings and begin to pray very specific prayers and make clear decrees for the coming of the kingdom of God on the earth.

The first thirteen verses of "The Gospel According to Mark" give a very brief account of the ministry of John the Baptist. In verse fourteen, Mark makes a shift to the coverage of the ministry of Jesus. Pay close attention to what he wrote:

"Now after John was put in prison, Jesus came to Galilee, preaching the gospel of the kingdom of God, and saying, 'The time is fulfilled, and the kingdom of God is at hand. Repent, and believe in the gospel.'" (Mark 1:14-15)

According to Mark, Jesus arrived in Galilee with a three part message. First, Jesus made a big announcement, "The time is fulfilled!" We have to study to understand what Jesus meant when He made that announcement, but the people of that day readily understood his meaning. People in the region of Galilee would have understood this to mean a fulfillment of the messianic prophecies which had reemerged after John the Baptist made his appearance. John had clearly announced that he was "the voice crying out in the wilderness." His mission was to prepare the way for the arrival of Messiach.

Jesus' words would have been received as a declaration that Messiach had arrived. People had long been in prayer asking God to make it happen. Modern day intercessors are still crying out for the coming of the Messiah King. It is clearly a part of our prayer mission to seek the second coming of Jesus Christ as King of kings and Lord of lords.

The second part of Jesus' message was a call to repentance. This validated the ministry and message of John the Baptist. Note that when Jesus proclaimed the call to repentance, it was being offered with a slightly different purpose. It was more than the preparation for the coming Messiah announced by John. Jesus was calling people to repent in preparation for entering the kingdom of God which was already at hand.

In the spirit of John the Baptist (the Elijah spirit) we continue to pray with many prayers of intercession for the world to repent in order to prepare a way into the wilderness of their hearts in order to receive Jesus as savior. And, in the spirit of Jesus, we are calling people to repentance in order to be ready to enter the kingdom of God right now. Both are very present needs for people who want to be welcomed into the kingdom of God. Father God wants all His children to come home and live eternally in His kingdom. It is our task to put our authority in prayer behind the Father's will in order to bring them to Him. We need to continue to cry out for people, nations, and the world to repent and get back into right relationship with our creator God and Father.

The third part of Jesus' message was a call for people to believe the gospel. It is not enough to just hear it. People need to believe it wholeheartedly. After almost two thousand years of preaching, people seem further away from faith than at any time in the past. People today are openly mocking God on TV, the internet, and in newspapers. I believe that one of the reasons for our current state is that during the last couple of centuries the church moved away from its purpose and only focused on the first part of the gospel. The church has been proclaiming the gospel of salvation more than the gospel of the kingdom of God. There is a difference.

The message about salvation is extremely important. Salvation is the doorway into the kingdom. However the gospel of the kingdom goes further. It continues with the preaching of kingdom principles and Godly values to the disciples of every generation and to spread the gospel to the ends of the earth.

Each soul is extremely important to Father God and we should never minimize the value of someone accepting salvation and being born again. It is wonderful! However, as intercessors and disciples we want more. We are to disciple nations so that we can bring the world back to Father God. We have gotten lost in the weeds and have to strain to see the entire vision. Intercessor warriors are praying specific and powerful prayers for the nations to come to the Lord.

Matthew gave an expanded version of the mission as he documents Jesus' teaching about prayer.

*"This, then, is how you should pray: 'Our Father in heaven, hallowed be your name, **your kingdom come**, your will be done on earth as it is in heaven. Give us today our daily bread. Forgive us our debts, as we also have forgiven our debtors. And lead us not into temptation, but deliver us from the evil one. For if you forgive men when they sin against you, your heavenly Father will also forgive you. But if you do not forgive men their sins, your Father will not forgive your sins.'"* (Matthew 6:9-15, NIV)

Jesus taught the disciples to pray for God's will to *"be done on earth as it is in heaven."* This is a prayer which we need to sincerely bring before the Lord over and over. The earth is far from seeing these results. Many churches do not cry out and seek for "the will of God" to be done in their membership; much less the world. This is an area for our continued intercessory prayers. There are two powerful reasons for us to do this: we really need it and the Lord commanded us to do it.

The Lord said that we are to be praying for people to be delivered from evil. Yet many churches refuse to have deliverance ministries or deliverance services. No wonder evil is on the move. All that evil needs in order to expand is for righteous people to do nothing. Jesus commanded us to cast out demons.

"And as you go, preach, saying, 'The kingdom of heaven is at hand.' Heal the sick, cleanse the lepers, raise the dead, cast out demons. Freely you have received, freely give." (Matthew 10:7-8)

Clearly, it is an appropriate kingdom prayer to seek deliverance for all who are oppressed by the devil. From this command from Jesus, we see that there are three other things we should be praying to manifest as the kingdom of God comes on the earth. We should pray for the dead to be raise, the sick to be healed, and lepers to be cleansed.

I have saved the most difficult part of Jesus' teaching of kingdom prayers for last, because I have experienced that so many people resent this message and simply refuse to obey. Jesus said,

> *"Forgive us our debts, as we also have forgiven our debtors. And lead us not into temptation, but deliver us from the evil one. For if you forgive men when they sin against you, your heavenly Father will also forgive you. But if you do not forgive men their sins, your Father will not forgive your sins."*

Did you notice that this part of the prayer is much longer than all the rest combined? Jesus knew how much difficulty we would have with this kind of kingdom prayer. I believe that is why He gave so much space to this teaching here and in many other passages.

It is very important for us to learn to ask for people to be forgiven when they have injured or offended us. We cannot ask God to forgive us of every debt while refusing to forgive a simple unintended offense. When we hold un-forgiveness in our hearts, we block the flow of the blessing of the Lord in our own lives. Even more tragically, we jeopardize our own forgiveness from Father God. Study Jesus' teachings on these things. He brought it up over and over because it is so critically important. Read aloud the passage below and accept it as a part of your walk of faith.

> *"And whenever you stand praying, if you have anything against anyone, forgive him, that your Father in heaven may also forgive you your trespasses. But if you do not forgive, neither will your Father in heaven forgive your trespasses."* (Mark 11:25-26)

As you consider these teachings by Jesus, think about what He told the Pharisees concerning the coming of the kingdom of God.

> *"Now when He was asked by the Pharisees when the kingdom of God would come, He answered them and said, "The kingdom of God does not come with observation; nor will they say, 'See here!' or 'See there!' For indeed, <u>the kingdom of God is within you</u>."* (Luke 17:20-21)

If you have a grasp on the need to forgive before the judgment, think about how important it is right now, because the kingdom of God is already inside you. What you tolerate in your own spirit, you are releasing in the kingdom of God. I don't want un-forgiveness to be loosed in the kingdom of God. How about you? This is perhaps the most important area of our prayers for the kingdom of God to come. How many times has it been held up because of the evil in the hearts of so called believers?

PRAYING FOR CITIZENS OF THE KINGDOM

> *"Now, therefore, you are no longer strangers and foreigners, but fellow citizens with the saints and members of the household of God, having been built on the foundation of the apostles and prophets, Jesus Christ Himself being the chief cornerstone, in whom the whole building, being fitted together, grows into a holy temple in the Lord, in whom you also are being built together for a dwelling place of God in the Spirit."* (Ephesians 2:19-22)

Notice first that the kingdom is build on a strong foundation. The prophets and apostles are some of the stones and Jesus is the chief cornerstone. This is a wonderful and sound foundation for the entire body of believers and it is the very solid and permanent foundation for each of our spiritual houses. We not only have the holy temple of the Lord, but we ourselves are also a temple for God.

Next, notice the idea of citizenship. Citizenship is important. In most modern cultures, there are certain rights and privileges that come with citizenship. We like the benefits, but there is more to the story. Along with the privileges, come certain responsibilities. Many people have a difficult time accepting this aspect of citizenship. For example, I have not met very many people who like to pay taxes or obey complex rules and guidelines they didn't help to establish.

"Jesus answered and said to him, 'Most assuredly, I say to you, unless one is born again, he cannot see the kingdom of God.'" (John 3:3)

There is something very unique about citizenship in the kingdom of God. It is like an adoption. You are at the same time a citizen and a member of the royal family. This is such a powerful concept that Jesus describes it as being born again. You don't just get moved into the kingdom. You are born again as a new creation into His established kingdom. You get a fresh start! You begin at the top instead of at the bottom. You have full citizenship immediately. You are instantly a part of the family of God. You have an inheritance and a great benefits package.

One of our great tasks as intercessors is to pray for people to be born again. At times these prayers are needed for people who are already members of churches but have not entered the kingdom family as of yet. This is made more difficult by an emerging resentment over the idea of "being born again." Some people, even some long time church members, see this as excluding people from the kingdom of God and they believe it is something shameful. This is partially due to some poor teaching and ineffective modeling in the past, but also because so many people are unfamiliar with God's Word.

Jesus clearly says, this is the only way in. He didn't say it to exclude people, but to show them the entrance and welcome them to all the privileges and benefits of membership. We have an uphill battle against public opinion on this matter. Our prayer focus needs to be on people and not on political issues. Much intercessory prayer is needed in this area.

When you pray for citizens of the kingdom, you are praying for those who are already citizens and those you are inviting in. It is time for the intercessors to cry out on behalf of all those who have not yet received the new birth.

A large part of our healing ministry is for those who are already members of the household of God. James gives us a good model for this kind of prayer.

"Is anyone among you suffering? Let him pray. Is anyone cheerful? Let him sing psalms. Is anyone among you sick? Let him call for the elders of the church, and let them pray over him, anointing him with oil in the name of the Lord. And the prayer of faith will save the sick, and the Lord will raise him up. And if he has committed sins, he will be forgiven. Confess your trespasses to one another, and pray for one another, that you may be healed. The effective, fervent prayer of a righteous man avails much." (James 5:13-16)

This passage is directed at people who are already in the kingdom, but have needs for healing in all three areas of their being: spirit, soul, and body. James gives us a variety of prayer techniques for different types of problems. I believe that we all like the final sentence in this passage: *"The effective, fervent prayer of a righteous man (or woman) avails much.*

As citizens of the kingdom may we stand in agreement to pray for one another at all times. May we join together in a shared ministry of love and grace! May we pour out our hearts before Father God daily asking for his help for our brothers and sisters in the kingdom!

PRAYING FOR THE SPREAD OF THE GOSPEL OF THE KINGDOM

"And He said, '*The kingdom of God is as if a man should scatter seed on the ground, and should sleep by night and rise by day, and the seed should sprout and grow, he himself does not know how. For the earth yields crops by itself: first the blade, then the head, after that the full grain in the head. But when the grain ripens, immediately he puts in the sickle, because the harvest has come.*'" (Mark 4:26-29)

I am a sower! How about you? Most often people read this passage and immediately think of sowing and reaping in terms of money. Many messages have been given before the offering at church or in evangelistic meetings about sowing seeds into the kingdom. There is nothing wrong with these messages. They are truthful teachings. However, we do not serve the kingdom well if we only use them for fund raising. In these parables, Jesus identified the seed as the Word of God. Jesus is talking about spreading the gospel of the kingdom in the way that a farmer would spread seed over the field. Jesus is focused on a harvest of souls for the kingdom of God.

In contemporary times, it has become more convenient to feel good about giving money to the pastor or evangelist with the expectation that they will do the work and you will share in the rewards. This is true, but it is not a completely honest presentation of the gospel. Jesus expanded this thought when he proclaimed the gospel of the kingdom. He was calling then and is still calling for people to volunteer to be workers in the fields in order to bring in a harvest of souls for the kingdom of God.

"Now when it was day, He departed and went into a deserted place. And the crowd sought Him and came to Him, and tried to keep Him from leaving them; but He said to them, 'I must preach the kingdom of God to the other cities also, because for this purpose I have been sent.'" (Luke 4:42-43)

It is human nature to want the focus of the presence of God to be on us. People sought for Jesus to stay with them so that more could be healed, taught, and blessed. They wanted a corner on the market of Jesus' presence. But Jesus had a clear vision of His ministry. He had to take it as far as He could in the time He had. He sensed the urgency because He knew that there was not much time.

Most of us have difficulty holding to an awareness of how short the time is. However like Jesus we need to be concerned about the spread of the kingdom. Like Jesus we do not want even one soul to be lost. Kingdom intercessors stay focused and are alert to the shortness of times as they pray for the lost, and the spread of the gospel of the kingdom. Have you received this call? Do you sense the urgency? Are you actively praying for the lost to be saved?

"Then He said, 'To what shall we liken the kingdom of God? Or with what parable shall we picture it? It is like a mustard seed which, when it is sown on the ground, is smaller than all the seeds on earth; but when it is sown, it grows up and becomes greater than all herbs, and shoots out large branches, so that the birds of the air may nest under its shade.'" (Mark 4:30-32)

I love this teaching. Most churches are overly focused on the size of their membership. Some think that a small congregation means a ministry has failed. At times, we seek more numbers with greater intensity than we seek the depth of kingdom commitment.

In spite of what the Lord said through the prophet Zechariah, people do despise the day of small things. Jesus points us to the mustard seed to understand what can happen when we sow the Word in kingdom fields. The plant grows larger than bushes and shrubs. The Lord can take our small beginnings, little offerings, a slight work and expand them into a mighty move for the kingdom. Pray now that the Lord will raise up another man or woman in the spirit of Evan Roberts, Maria Woodworth-Etter, or William Seymour. Pray for workers to be called to the harvest.

"But when Jesus saw it, He was greatly displeased and said to them, 'Let the little children come to Me, and do not forbid them; for of such is the kingdom of God. Assuredly, I say to you, whoever does not receive the kingdom of God as a little child will by no means enter it.' And He took them up in His arms, laid His hands on them, and blessed them." (Mark 10:14-16)

Pray for all the adults in the kingdom of God to be more like little children. Pray for everyone to have the sincere faith of a little child. Pray that all would be as innocent and unassuming as the children we love. Imagine what could happen if we prayed for the things Jesus has already told us are the will of Father God.

"And again He said, 'To what shall I liken the kingdom of God? It is like leaven, which a woman took and hid in three measures of meal till it was all leavened.'" (Luke 13:20-21)

As dough rises when we add active yeast, I hope and pray for the kingdom of God to begin to swell and reach its full potential. May it spread like leaven throughout the entire earth so that all have an opportunity to respond to the gospel of the kingdom! Amen and Amen!

PRAYING ACCORDING TO KINGDOM PRINCIPLES

"Therefore do not worry, saying, 'What shall we eat?' or 'What shall we drink?' or 'What shall we wear?' For after all these things the Gentiles seek. For your heavenly Father knows that you need all these things. But seek first the kingdom of God and His righteousness, and all these things shall be added to you. Therefore do not worry about tomorrow, for tomorrow will worry about its own things. Sufficient for the day is its own trouble." (Matthew 6:31-34)

One powerful kingdom principle is that Father God already knows what you need. He doesn't need a daily laundry list of things for Him to do on our behalf. If you add to this notion that He has your best interests at heart, it should change how you prayer. You no longer have to cry out for every little human need. You can focus your prayers on kingdom missions. Remember: the kingdom doesn't really spread because of your many well thought out words. How does it spread? Hear what Paul said in 1 Corinthians 4:20, *"For the kingdom of God is not in word but in power."* Pray for the power of God to be released in our area of the kingdom. Praying like that will accomplish more than all your words.

It is a kingdom principle that we are to be given wisdom and revelation so that we have understanding of all the mysteries of the kingdom. To accomplish this kingdom mission, the Lord sent the Spirit of truth to guide you in all truth. Ask for His help and let Him work in and through you! Amen!

> *"And He said to them, 'To you it has been given to know the mystery of the kingdom of God; but to those who are outside, all things come in parables, so that Seeing they may see and not perceive, And hearing they may hear and not understand; Lest they should turn, And their sins be forgiven them.'"* (Mark 4:11-12)

Another principle I really like concerns kingdom math. Kingdom math is always multiplication and not just addition. When you operate in kingdom authority, and pray from that position you should expect hundred fold results. If you think this is too ambitious look again at what Jesus taught.

> *"So Jesus answered and said, 'Assuredly, I say to you, there is no one who has left house or brothers or sisters or father or mother or wife or children or lands, for My sake and the gospel's, who shall not receive a <u>hundredfold now in this time</u>—houses and brothers and sisters and mothers and children and lands, with persecutions—and in the age to come, eternal life.'"* (Mark 10:29-30)

Another kingdom principle concerns the role of faith. Everything is based on faith. Nothing works without it and nothing is impossible with it. How much faith do you need? Actually you only need a little as long as you don't try to mix doubt in with it.

> *"So Jesus answered and said to them, 'Assuredly, I say to you, <u>if you have faith</u> and do not doubt, you will not only do what was done to the fig tree, but also if you say to this mountain, 'Be removed and be cast into the sea,'*

it will be done. And whatever things you <u>ask in prayer</u>, <u>believing</u>, you will receive.'" (Matthew 21:21-22)

KINGDOM BINDING AND LOOSING

"Jesus answered and said to him, 'Blessed are you, Simon Bar-Jonah, for flesh and blood has not revealed this to you, but My Father who is in heaven. And I also say to you that you are Peter, and on this rock I will build My church, and the gates of Hades shall not prevail against it. And I will give you the keys of the kingdom of heaven, and <u>whatever you bind</u> on earth will be bound in heaven, and <u>whatever you loose</u> on earth will be loosed in heaven.'" (Matthew 16:17-19)

Binding and loosing in the kingdom of God is an awesome responsibility. Most of us like the idea that we can bind things on earth. There are many things which need binding and we have been given the authority to do it. What most people are unsure about is binding things in heaven. Many people ask me how this is possible. Who has that kind of authority in heaven? What right do I have to bind things in heaven? These are tough questions and we need answers.

We also like the message about being able to loose things on earth. There are many people, organizations, and programs which need to be loosed on earth. Many people and churches need to be loosed from the religious spirit and freed from being in bondage to outdated manmade doctrines. Many church groups need to be loosed from their bonds to past programs which everyone fears changing. That brings up another thing we need to be loosed from – a spirit of fear. So many things would move forward if we could just get ourselves and our congregations, and our prayer groups free from this spirit of fear. But who has the authority to loose things in heaven? How can you do that?

As I was writing the Lord gave me a revelation about this. Put all of this in the context of what Jesus taught in Luke chapter 17:

> *"Now when He was asked by the Pharisees when the kingdom of God would come, He answered them and said, "The kingdom of God does not come with obser-vation; nor will they say, 'See here!' or 'See there!' For indeed, <u>the kingdom of God is within you</u>."* (Luke 17:20-21)

When you loose things for others in your ministry, you also loose them within yourself. When you bind things in others, you also bind them in yourself. This is a wonderful privilege for kingdom citizens who are true disciples of Jesus Christ. A kingdom principle is that with great privilege comes great responsibility. We have to avoid every temptation to err in what we bind and loose. We must be aware that there are incorrect kinds of binding and loosing.

> *"But woe to you, scribes and Pharisees, hypocrites! For you shut up the kingdom of heaven against men; for you neither go in yourselves, nor do you allow those who are entering to go in."* (Matthew 23:13)

Believe me, you don't want to receive a "woe" statement from Jesus. You don't want to hear Him call you a "hypocrite!" The enemy wants us to bind people in a way that will limit their kingdom authority and benefits. If we react out of hurt or offense, we are likely to make this really big mistake. We must never shut the door to the kingdom of heaven for another person. We don't clearly see the big picture of God's plan for others. Even if they have been caught in sin, the Lord may have a clear plan to lead them to repentance and restoration.

Study Paul's teaching about eating meat as a lesson about inappropriate binding and loosing. You must learn these lessons well so that you never receive a "Woe to you" from Jesus. We are not to loose things in people which are in a weak area of temptation which might lead them back into sin or an immoral lifestyle. We must be as careful about inappropriate loosing as we are about incorrect binding.

STANDING ON THE STONE OF THE KINGDOM

This has been a quick look at the "Foundation Stone of the Kingdom." There is so much more to this. I hope that this has inspired you to search further and develop a belief system much deeper than I have been able to provide here. Continue to ask the Holy Spirit for wisdom and understanding, council and might, understanding and the fear of the Lord (Isaiah 11:2).

Continue to examine yourself. Are you firmly standing on the foundation stone of the kingdom of God? If not, do whatever it takes to get back on the solid foundation as soon as possible.

May the Lord bless you as you move up in your calling as an intercessor warrior!

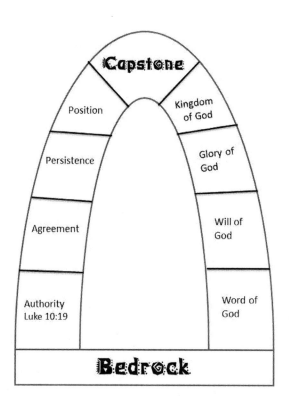

Kingdom of God: The Eight Stone in the Foundation

CHAPTER 9

THE CAPSTONE – JESUS CHRIST

"So this is what the Sovereign Lord says: "See, I lay a stone in Zion, a tested stone, a precious cornerstone for a sure foundation; the one who trusts will never be dismayed." (Isaiah 28:16, NIV)

*I*n the beginning, I mentioned my struggle with picturing a foundation with and odd number of stones. When the Lord first gave this revelation to me, I was shown five stones for the foundation. At that time, I prepared and preached a five part sermon series on the foundation stones for intercessory prayer. About a year later, the Lord gave me a revelation of two more stones. Reflecting on the prophetic meaning of the number seven, I decided that this was the complete picture and named this book, "Seven Foundation Stones for Intercessor Warriors." However in the spring of this year as I was teaching this in a conference in Chicago the Lord gave me a revelation of two more stones. In the Bible, the number nine means divine perfection. This revelation came shortly after the Lord began to speak to me about restoring foundations. Putting these two revelations together, I renamed the book: "Restoring Foundations for Intercessor Warriors."

The Biblical picture of the cornerstone has been with us for thousands of years. Isaiah prophesied about the coming Messiah and understood that He would be the sure foundation for all those who are established in the Lord. If you want your faith and future to be built on a sure foundation, Jesus must be the cornerstone for you.

"He will be the sure foundation for your times, a rich store of salvation and wisdom and knowledge; the fear of the Lord is the key to this treasure." (Isaiah 33:6, NIV)

I accepted this by faith in God and in the prophetic messages given and made manifest in His Word. But, I still didn't understand how to make a "4 square" foundation with five, seven, or nine stones.

When the Lord started speaking to me about restoring the foundations, I clearly understood that prayer is an integral part of the foundation, but it is not the entire foundation. As I sought help from the Lord to understand more about restoring foundations, He brought me back to the revelation I had received almost two years earlier. He reminded me again that Jesus is the cornerstone for the entire foundation. At the same time, he is the cornerstone of this part of the foundation. But, I still had difficulty picturing it in my mind.

When we visited in Israel, it all became clear. That massive stone foundation doesn't actually rest on the ground. To understand why, you have to understand some Jewish beliefs. It is a foundational concept in their theology that the bones of people defile the ground. The Temple could not rest on ground where bones might be buried. But how could they build it any other way. In the outpouring of wisdom given by God, Solomon understood how to do it. The floor of the Temple could be built so that any part which was not on bedrock would actually be suspended in the air. At first this is difficult to imagine, because of the tremendous amount of weight from all the other stones. Solomon saw that by building a complex system of stone arches anchored on the bedrock below they could protect the Temple from actually coming into direct contact with the soil.

This was the missing piece of the revelation for me. Now I understood what the Lord had been saying to me. An arch is made of an uneven number of stones. When the stones are formed into two ascending columns, an even number of stones are needed to build it up to the desire height. Then, the last stone is added. This stone is called the capstone (a lynchpin). This stone is normally shaped like a wedge, and its weight places pressure on the two columns which actually gives them increased strength. The pressure from the weight of this stone actually holds it all together. This is the message in these prophetic words. The person of Jesus Christ holds the foundation together. It is His weighty presence pressing down on the rest of the body which provides the strength and stability for us to continue to stand. Jesus is the lynchpin (capstone or cornerstone) of this supportive structure.

When they built the Temple, they faced many difficult challenges requiring revelation knowledge from the Lord. Here is another interesting spiritual problem they faced: the Ark could not sit on a dressed stone. The Lord provided the answer when He led David to the threshing floor of Araunah. In those days a threshing floor was made of a large flat rock with enough surface area for people to complete the tasks for getting the soft content of the grain out of the thick and tough husks.

Protruding through the dressed stones of the Temple Mount are two large natural stones. One is believed to be Mount Moriah where Abraham went in order to sacrifice Isaac. The blue Mosque is build over that stone and it is now unavailable to all non-Muslim visitors to the Temple Mount. The other stone is in the center of the large open area on the foundation of this structure. Many scholars believed it to be the threshing floor of Araunah where David built an altar to stop the plague on Israel, and it is highly likely that the Temple was built over this stone. It is also believed by many to be the actual location of the Holy of Holies. This theory is based on the belief that the Ark of the Covenant with the Mercy Seat on top was placed on this stone.

> *"And Gad came that day to David and said to him, "Go up, erect an altar to the Lord on the threshing floor of Araunah the Jebusite."* (2 Samuel 24:18)

In ancient Jewish literature it is written that the Temple was to be built on a line which could be drawn from the Mount of Olives over the Golden Gate to this very spot. The blue Mosque does not fit this description. It is far off of this line. So the logical conclusion is that the Temple was located in this spot. The stone threshing floor of Araunah is a part of the bedrock under this site, and there is no possibility of bones being under it to defile the sacred structures. Only the Lord could weave all this together for us.

HOW THIS RELATES
TO INTERCESSORY PRAYER

> *"Consequently, you are no longer foreigners and aliens, but fellow citizens with God's people and members of God's household, built on the foundation of the apostles and prophets, with Christ Jesus himself as the chief cornerstone. In him the whole building is joined together and rises to become a holy temple in the Lord. And in him you too are being built together to become a dwelling in which God lives by his Spirit."* (Ephesians 2:19-22, NIV)

Consider first the strong New Testament teaching about the Temple of God. Paul and others establish clearly on the written and revealed Word of God that you and I are the temple of the Lord today.

> *"Don't you know that <u>you yourselves are God's temple</u> and that God's Spirit lives in you? If anyone destroys God's temple, God will destroy him; for <u>God's temple is sacred</u>, and <u>you are that temple</u>."* (1 Corinthians 3:16-17, NIV)

All of these ideas about the creative and extensive building of the physical Temple on Earth is actually about you as the Temple of God. Like Solomon's Temple, you need a strong foundation made up of hewn stones, large stones, and precious stones. The Lord is building you up with His own materials and on His established foundation so that you are cleansed and not defiled as His temple. The Lord has done it and it is awesome.

The most precious of all stones was provided for you at great cost. It is a both a precious and a costly stone.

> *"Haven't you read this scripture: 'The stone the builders rejected has become the capstone; the Lord has done this, and it is marvelous in our eyes'?"* (Mark 12:10-11, NIV)

Here you can notice that with more modern translations this stone is being identified as the *"capstone."* This fits in with what the Lord has been revealing to me over the past three years, but I didn't see it until I saw the actual foundation of the Temple in Jerusalem. Jesus is the capstone of the arch supporting you and me as His temple. Here is an amazing and awesome thought: The Lord has done this for us, and it truly is marvelous in our eyes! Amen?

What is true for the entire temple foundation is true for each part. Jesus is the capstone of the temple and He is also the capstone of your foundation as an intercessor warrior. This was not a new idea when Jesus taught it during His time of ministry. When He gave this teaching, Jesus was quoting word for word from the book of Psalms.

"The stone the builders rejected has become the cap-stone; the LORD has done this, and it is marvelous in our eyes." (Psalm 118:22-23, NIV)

It is a *"marvelous"* Word from the Lord and it is awesome to know that the Lord Himself is holding you up, supporting you, giving you strength and permanence, and releasing power to uphold you now and forever.

Jesus holds us up in so many marvelous ways. He is holding your needs up before the Lord. The capstone of your foundation is also your intercessor before Father God and is praying constantly for you and all who belong to Him. Read aloud the words Paul gave to the church in Rome and make it yours.

"Who is he who condemns? It is Christ who died, and furthermore is also risen, who is even at the right hand of God, who also makes intercession for us." (Romans 8:34)

At this point I would like to expand this concept even further. The foundation has already been built and yet it is still being built up. You don't need any new stones. You just need to get back on the ones which have already been provided. Then make it a commitment to never get off of this foundation. Considering this, you need to understand that this is an ongoing project. You are the Temple of God and yet you are at the same time still becoming His temple. Look closely at how Peter taught this concept.

"As you come to him, the living Stone—rejected by men but chosen by God and precious to him—you also, like

living stones, are <u>being built</u> into a spiritual house to be a holy priesthood, offering spiritual sacrifices acceptable to God through Jesus Christ. (1 Peter 2:4-5)

You are the Temple of God and yet you are still being built into a spiritual house where you will be part of the holy priesthood, ministering unto the Lord forever. Isn't that an amazing thought? But there is more! You are now enabled to offer spiritual sacrifices acceptable to God through Jesus! What are those sacrifices? I will not go into a great deal of detail here. That is for another study. In the meantime, you know that it is not a reestablishment of the sacrificial system. Jesus took care of that once and for all. What is an acceptable sacrifice to the Lord? Among other things consider this word from Paul:

"I beseech you therefore, brethren, by the mercies of God, that you present your bodies a living sacrifice, holy, acceptable to God, which is your reasonable service. And do not be conformed to this world, but be transformed by the renewing of your mind, that you may prove what is that good and acceptable and perfect will of God." (Romans 12:1-2)

I believe that Peter and Paul were both talking about this same idea of presenting ourselves as living sacrifices and then allowing the Lord to renew our minds in order to transform our souls, making us fit for service in the kingdom of God and ready to enter eternal life.

THIRD HEAVEN INTERCESSION

I am issuing a challenge to all the intercessors who have not already shifted from second Heaven intercession to Third Heaven intercession to do so now. We have moved into a new season of spiritual warfare, and we need to step away from the enemy's traps and move into the Secret Place of the Most High for our service as intercessor warriors. Too many intercessors have already suffered the effects of wrestling principalities outside their area of authority. The question for many is how do we make this shift? I believe the answer was given by the writer of the book of Hebrews.

"For we do not have a High Priest who cannot sympa-thize with our weaknesses, but was in all points tempted as we are, yet without sin. Let us therefore come boldly to the throne of grace, that we may obtain mercy and find grace to help in time of need. (Hebrews 4:15-16)

You may now go "boldly to the throne of grace." Where is this throne of grace? I have heard some really poor teaching on this topic. Most of these teachings tried to prove that this is not really true as stated. It is only talking about saying prayers. I totally disagree with these ideas. I believe that the writer of Hebrews meant exactly what he said. To understand this better, it is helpful to connect Hebrews 4:15-16 with Hebrews 8:1-2.

"Now this is the main point of the things we are saying: We have such a High Priest, who is seated at the right hand of the throne of the Majesty in the heavens, a Minister of the sanctuary and of the true tabernacle which the Lord erected, and not man." (Hebrews 8:1-2)

The throne of grace is located where Jesus resides with the Father right now. This passage makes it clear that it is in the Third Heaven. Now we understand that this is where Jesus is interceding for you and me. Jesus was the greatest of all the teachers who have ever lived on earth. He adopted the style of modeling what He taught. I believe what the writer of Hebrew said in chapter thirteen verse eight: *"Jesus Christ is the same yesterday, today, and forever."* If Jesus taught this way in the past, He is teaching the same way now and forever. He is now modeling what He taught about intercessory prayer. He is praying in the Third Heaven "*at the right hand of the throne of the Majesty*" of our Father God.

Consider these two facts: 1) Jesus chooses to intercede in this place; and 2) you have been called to take your prayers boldly to this same place: "before the throne of grace." It is clear to me that this is our best and proper place of interces- sion. Study the scriptures and draw your own conclusions. In the meantime, I will issue the challenge again for intercessors to lift up their prayers from their place in the Third Heaven. Another amazing thought: you are seated with Him in heaven. If you are a disciple of Jesus Christ you have a seat in this place.

> "*And God raised us up with Christ and seated us with him in the heavenly realms in Christ Jesus, in order that in the coming ages he might show the incomparable riches of his grace, expressed in his kindness to us in Christ Jesus.*" (Ephesians 2:6-7, NIV)

When you are seated in Heaven with Him, you experience a different level of communication. So few things have to be spoken, because you know that He knows everything you can ask or imagine long before you say it. You also know that He loves you and has your best interests in His heart. You know that He is already taking action on your behalf before you ask.

It just keeps getting better! You have the same access that Jesus has to Father God in Heaven. Do you have some doubts about this? Then consider Ephesians 2:18, "*For through him (Jesus) we both have access to the Father by one Spirit.*" If you are in Christ, you have access to the Father right alongside Jesus. Isn't that an amazing and wonderful thought? It is the truth! It is in the Word of God! God is now giving you above and beyond all you have asked or imagined.

But, there is one big qualifier. Do you really believe it? Remember that you only access those kingdom principles you actually believe in. If you don't believe you will be healed, guess what? You will not be healed! Your level of expectation based on faith is the key to receiving the promises of God. Jesus taught and modeled this. Consider what He said to the Roman Centurion:

"Then Jesus said to the centurion, "Go your way; and as you have believed, so let it be done for you." And his servant was healed that same hour." (Matthew 8:13)

Jesus said something very similar to this when He released healing power to two blind men. *"Then He touched their eyes, saying, 'According to your faith let it be to you.'"* (Matthew 9:29) They had faith and believed they would be healed, and they received just as Jesus said. How is your faith? Many times we get what we expect – nothing – and then we complain about it. It is time to build up your most holy faith. Are you unsure if you have "holy faith?" Consider this word from the book of Jude:

"But you, beloved, building yourselves up on your most holy faith, praying in the Holy Spirit, keep yourselves in the love of God, looking for the mercy of our Lord Jesus Christ unto eternal life." (Jude 1:20-21)

This is all amazing and wonderful, but it doesn't stop here. There is more – much more. Think about this: You are not only seated in heaven, but heaven is in you. Consider the passage below:

"Jesus replied, "If anyone loves me, he will obey my teaching. My Father will love him, and we will come to him and make our home with him." (John 14:23, NIV)

MORE GOOD NEWS — WE HAVE THE NAME

"Therefore God exalted him to the highest place and gave him the name that is above every name, that at the name of Jesus every knee should bow, in heaven and on earth and under the earth, and every tongue confess that Jesus Christ is Lord, to the glory of God the Father." (Philippians 2:9-11, NIV)

There is great power in the name of Jesus. Are you using His Name and the power in His Name fully?

"Then Peter said, 'Silver or gold I do not have, but what I have I give you. In the name of Jesus Christ of Nazareth, walk.'" (Acts 3:6)

I don't believe that we have fully grasped or operated in this power. One way you can test yourself is to ask: "Am I currently speaking healing authority and power with this degree of certainty?" If not, you haven't attained to this level yet.

We need to move in faith from asking "if" it can be done to decreeing that it will be done. I refer to this as being elevated to the level of "whatever." For a more complete explanation read the Summary to the book. Suffice it to say:

*"I tell you the truth, anyone who has faith in me will do what I have been doing. He will do even greater things than these, because I am going to the Father. And I will do **whatever** you ask in my name, so that the Son may bring glory to the Father. You may ask me for anything in my name, and I will do it."* (John 14:12-14, NIV)

Someone asked me: How much can you ask for? My answer: You can ask for anything in His name and it will be done. Notice the added clause "in His name." Are you asking for things which can be done in His Name? Can you find it in the Word of God? Is it in accordance with the will of God? Will it bring glory to Jesus and Father God? Will it help to bring His kingdom into reality on earth as it is in Heaven? When you meet these criteria, it really is in His Name!

Perhaps you have your doubts. Maybe you need more evidence? Who are you going to trust? I trust Jesus more than anyone else! How about you? I also believe that this level is for disciples being led by the Holy Spirit and operating in the power of the Spirit. Listen to Peter's explanation:

> *"If we are being called to account today for an act of kindness shown to a cripple and are asked how he was healed, then know this, you and all the people of Israel: It is by the name of Jesus Christ of Nazareth, whom you crucified but whom God raised from the dead, that this man stands before you healed. He is 'the stone you builders rejected, which has become the capstone.'"*
> (Acts 4:9-11, NIV)

If you want to operate at the spiritual level of "whatever," you need to deepen your faith. It takes a deep level of spiritual belief to heal someone born lame. Peter's faith is so far beyond doubt that there is no hesitancy to speak up, decree healing, and testify to a resurrected Lord. It takes a profound trust in the Lord to go before the ruling council and proclaim the power of the name of Jesus only a few days after they put Him to death. Are you ready to operate at the spiritual level of "whatever?"

What are the limitations on using this name? You can't throw it around like the seven sons of Sceva who had no personal relationship with Jesus. You can't call yourself into an anointing. Your own personal skills, abilities, charm, and intellect will not bring a healing miracle to anyone. There is only one way to get it. There is only one source for authority and power to operate in the Spiritual gifts.

"You did not choose me, but I chose you and appointed you to go and bear fruit—fruit that will last. Then the Father will give you whatever you ask in my name." (John 15:16, NIV)

Jesus said, "whatever you ask in my name." When you have been chosen and appointed by Jesus to bear fruit that will last, the limitations are taken away and you can do what Jesus did and perhaps even more. Are you ready for it?

I believe that you need to take this faith further and further. That's what Jesus did. Each time He talked about it the level went higher. Jesus says that you can reach a level where you are allowed to go directly to the Father. You can do this because you belong to Jesus. His name has opened a doorway for you into the Father's presence. When that happens you can go directly to the Father, and the Father will give you "whatever you ask in my name." Notice that the name of Jesus is still the key, but you now have access to the Father. You can go boldly before the throne of Grace in the Third Heaven.

"In that day you will no longer ask me anything. I tell you the truth, my Father will give you whatever you ask in my name. Until now you have not asked for anything in my name. Ask and you will receive, and your joy will be complete." (John 16:23-24)

WHEN YOU NEED ASSURANCE, GO TO THE NAME

"These things I have written to you who believe in the name of the Son of God, that you may know that you have eternal life, and that you may continue to believe in the name of the Son of God." (1 John 5:13)

The name of Jesus and your faith brings the awesome power of God. Think about how much more you will receive when you add agreement to the formula. When you get into agreement with other believers the results are multiplied. Just try to imagine how much can happen when you get into agreement with the Father, the Son, and the Holy Spirit.

> *"Again, I tell you that if two of you on earth agree about anything you ask for, it will be done for you by my Father in heaven. For where two or three come together in my name, there am I with them."* (Matthew 18:19-20, NIV)

Agreeing together brings the awesome power of God. In addition, coming together in unity brings Jesus into your midst. Now you are not only in agreement with each other, but He is there in agreement as well. Now, you can take it up another notch. Listen to what Jesus said in John 14:23:

> *"Jesus answered and said to him, 'If anyone loves Me, he will keep My word; and My Father will love him, and We will come to him and make Our home with him.'"*

This is a power packed promise! You need to internalize it! When you stand in agreement and in obedience to Jesus, He comes to join your group. When He comes, He brings the Father with Him.

I hope that you have learned during this study how important it is to intercede as teams. The Lord put you into teams for a reason, and to encourage you to do that, He adds all these other powerful benefits. Joined together with one another, the Father, and Jesus you are on a truly awesome team.

Most intercessory teams I know have a recognized leader. That is a good thing. However, consider this: let Jesus be the head of your intercessory team. You still need people to do some of the tasks to organize and keep things moving, but not at the expense of replacing Jesus. He is the head of the church and should be the head of every committee and program.

This would certainly be enough if nothing else were to be added. But, it gets even better! The Holy Spirit is also a power team member of your intercessory team.

> *"In the same way, the Spirit helps us in our weakness. We do not know what we ought to pray for, but the Spirit himself intercedes for us with groans that words cannot express. And he who searches our hearts knows the mind of the Spirit, because the Spirit intercedes for the saints in accordance with God's will."* (Romans 8:26-27, NIV)

With all that the Lord has done for you and all that He has provided for your needs, how can you lose? It's time to start standing on the promises of the Word. It is time to cast off all fear and stand courageously in the battle for souls. Remember what the Lord has promised and stand on it in faith.

> *"'No weapon formed against you shall prosper, And every tongue which rises against you in judgment You shall condemn. This is the heritage of the servants of the Lord, And their righteousness is from Me," Says the Lord."* (Isaiah 54:17)

Begin to stand in the authority Jesus gave you!

> *"I have given you authority to trample on snakes and scorpions and to overcome all the power of the enemy; nothing will harm you."* (Luke 10:19)

What can harm you? NOTHING! Right? Take what the Lord has given you and begin to make strong decrees that you will not fear. Get filled with the perfect love of Jesus because fear cannot remain in the Lord's domain.

"Love has been perfected among us in this: that we may have boldness in the day of judgment; because as He is, so are we in this world. There is no fear in love; but perfect love casts out fear, because fear involves torment. But he who fears has not been made perfect in love. We love Him because He first loved us." (1 John 4:17-19)

For these gifts from the Lord to work, you have to receive them, believe them, stand in them, and stand on them. Don't ever give up! Don't ever give in! When you've done everything to stand, keep on standing!

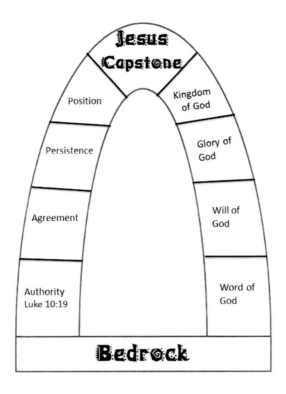

The Capstone: The Ninth Stone in the Foundation

SUMMARY

How can you make this permanent in your spiritual walk? There are some steps clearly outlined in the Word of God. Identify the principles associated with this anointing and begin to make decrees (over and over) based on these precepts. People often ask, "How long do you keep it up?" My answer is simple, "Keep it up as long as it takes!" Keep it up until it becomes second nature and it is the first action you take. Then learn the final lesson of the prophet Elisha!

"Now Elisha was suffering from the illness from which he died. Jehoash king of Israel went down to see him and wept over him. 'My father! My father!' he cried. 'The chariots and horsemen of Israel!' Elisha said, 'Get a bow and some arrows,' and he did so. 'Take the bow in your hands,' he said to the king of Israel. When he had taken it, Elisha put his hands on the king's hands. 'Open the east window,' he said, and he opened it. 'Shoot!' Elisha said, and he shot. 'The Lord's arrow of victory, the arrow of victory over Aram!' Elisha declared. 'You will completely destroy the Arameans at Aphek.' Then he said, 'Take the arrows,' and the king took them. Elisha told him, 'Strike the ground.' He struck it three times and stopped. The man of God was angry with him and said, 'You should have struck the ground five or six

times; then you would have defeated Aram and completely destroyed it. But now you will defeat it only three times.'" (2 Kings 13:14-19, NIV)

The king of Israel was only half-hearted when he struck the ground with the arrows. His heart was not in it, and it spoke of a lack of faith deep inside his soul. You must not be like that. Don't do things halfway. If you don't put your entire heart, soul, and faith into it you will only win a few little battles, but you may lose the war. Instead, make sure that you whole heartedly commit to destroying the works of the devil. This was Jesus mission and it is yours if you are His disciple. Any lack of faith erodes the power of God's promises in you. *"If you will not believe, Surely you shall not be established."* (Isaiah 7:9b)

"So they rose early in the morning and went out into the Wilderness of Tekoa; and as they went out, Jehoshaphat stood and said, "Hear me, O Judah and you inhabitants of Jerusalem: Believe in the Lord your God, and you shall be established; believe His prophets, and you shall prosper." (2 Chronicles 20:20)

Jehoshaphat knew that there were two keys to his success on the battlefield. He and his people had to have absolute faith in God. He had also learned to trust in the words of the prophets of the Lord. He came to this strong stance where he knew the secret of success. You get established in the Lord through your beliefs. You prosper through your faith.

Faith is a rare thing in many areas of the church. What most people call faith is little more than acknowledging that God exists. This is not enough faith to carry you to victory in spiritual warfare. If you don't add faith to your prayers, you are wasting your time and God's time. So, beware of the curse of double-mindedness!

"But when he asks, he must believe and not doubt, because he who doubts is like a wave of the sea, blown and tossed by the wind. That man should not think he will receive anything from the Lord; he is a double–minded man, unstable in all he does." (James 1:6-8, NIV)

Has anyone ever told you that believing is hard work? Consider what Jesus said in John 6:29, *"Jesus answered, 'The work of God is this: to believe in the one he has sent.'"* It is work, and it is your task! I want you to be built up in your most holy faith. To do so you must apply yourself and work at it. Even though it truly is a gift, you don't really possess it unless you work at it. Some things you have to do for yourself. Remember what Jude taught: *"But you, dear friends, build yourselves up in your most holy faith and pray in the Holy Spirit."* (Jude 1:20, NIV)

How do we get built up in faith? You have to work at it. *"So then faith comes by hearing, and hearing by the word of God."* (Romans 10:17)

"And this is his command: to believe in the name of his Son, Jesus Christ, and to love one another as he commanded us. Those who obey his commands live in him, and he in them. And this is how we know that he lives in us: We know it by the Spirit he gave us." (1 John 3:23-24)

ELEVATED TO THE LEVEL OF "WHATEVER"

As I was preparing to teach at a church in Korea, I heard the Lord say, "I am going to elevate them to the level of 'whatever.'" When I received this word from the Lord, I was more than a little surprised. The first thing that came to mind was a teenager answering with exasperation in his voice, "Whatever." This is used most often to stop the conversation. It is a put down which tells the speaker that you just don't care what they have to say or what they want. When you get this response, you know that whatever you have asked someone to do is not going to get done. I prayed and said, "Lord, I'm going to need a little help with this one. He gave me a scripture for His answer:

> *"Therefore I tell you, <u>whatever you ask for in prayer,</u> <u>**believe**</u> that you have received it, and <u>it will be yours</u>. And when you stand praying, if you hold anything against anyone, forgive him, so that your Father in heaven may forgive you your sins."* (Mark 11:24-25, NIV)

Do you want to be elevated to the level of "whatever?" I know that I wanted it after hearing this Word from the Lord. There are some steps you need to take if you want this elevation.

The spiritual season has shifted, and we can no longer just do business as usual. We have moved into a season of the manifestation of the Glory of God. You need to understand that when the Spirit of Glory comes, the Lord takes charge! Healing just happens in the Glory! People are being healed, creative miracles are manifesting! Everywhere we go, we are seeing people get healed without anointing oil or the laying on of hands. Without striving and contending, things are just happening in the Glory.

I celebrate what the Lord is doing, but I still wondered why? I heard the Lord saying that He isn't sharing His glory with any man or woman! When miracles happen and people get healed and restored without human efforts, we know that it is Him and no other! I want to say it again, we've moved into a time of His Glory!

The challenge now is: "How do we host the Glory?" The first thing the Lord revealed to me is that we need to ask for it – cry out for it – seek it in faith.

When it started to manifest in almost all our meetings, I asked the Lord, What can I do to bring your Glory Presence? The Lord said, "Praise my Name!" I didn't waste any time. Immediately after hearing this, I started with Psalm 103:1-5. I paraphrased it to be in the first person and I started saying it aloud over and over.

> *"Bless the Lord, O my soul; And all that is within me, bless His holy name! Bless the Lord, O my soul, And forget not all His benefits: Who forgives all my iniquities, Who heals all my diseases, Who redeems my life from destruction, Who crowns me with loving-kindness and tender mercies, Who satisfies my mouth with good things, So that my youth is renewed like the eagle's."*

God is so faithful. His Glory came and it was stronger and heavier than before! It was awesome. The next day I wanted more and I prayed for more. I wanted to be elevated to the level of "whatever" that Jesus talked about in Mark 11:24, *"Therefore I tell you, **whatever you ask** for in prayer, believe that you have received it, and it will be yours."*

Standing in faith on this promise I prayed for more – more of His glory – more of His weighty presence – more of His power. I asked again what I need to do to receive the answer to this prayer. The lord said, "Bless my name in Hebrew!"

In Israel, we connected with a Messianic pastor and spent quite a bit of time with him during the 2010 Hanukkah season. Because Jewish people do not say the name of God, they say, "Barukh ha Shem!" This means blessed be His Name! It is their version of "Praise the Lord!" Over several days the pastor had us saying it too. So, I just started saying "Barukh ha Shem!" over and over, and the Glory of God came again and was stronger than before. It was awesome.

A couple of days later, I prayed for still more! I was really going for the level of "whatever" in my prayer life.

This year, one of the Bibles I am studying is the Complete Jewish Bible. I read the passage in which the Lord revealed the true meaning of the Passover Seder to the disciples. In the Bibles I had read before it simply said that Jesus blessed the bread and the cup. But in the Jewish Bible it said, He gave the "Barukha!" This blessing is still used in Passover Seder meals today. The blessings for the bread and the wine go like this:

"Barukh atah adonai eloheynu melekh ha'olam hamotzi lekhem min ha'aretz" (Blessed are You, O Lord our God, Ruler of the universe, who brings forth bread from the earth.)

"Barukh atah adonai eloheynu melekh ha'olam borey pri hagafen." (Blessed are You, O Lord our God, Ruler of the universe, who creates the fruit of the vine.)

I started to pray an abbreviated version of these daily. I prayed: "Barukh atah adonai eloheynu melekh ha'olam." (Blessed are You, O Lord our God, Ruler of the universe.) When I did this, more glory came. God is so faithful and so good. Simple things spoken in love, faith, worship, and expectancy seem to invoke His Presence. In doing these simple things there is no glory for us, so it gives all the glory to Him and it brings His Glory to us!

When the building of the temple was completed, they had a huge dedication ceremony. People sang a simple praise song: *"For He is good, For His mercy endures forever"* (2 Chronicles 7:3) The only thing unique about the way they sang was that it was done with such unity that all the voices and all the instruments made "one sound." Simple praise mixed with the law of agreement brought a powerful outpouring of His Glory.

The cloud of His Presence filled the temple! The priests could no longer serve because His glory was too weighty for them to continue to stand! When the Glory came all of Solomon's prayers were answered. The Lord is so awesome, and amazing healings, signs and wonders accompany His Glory. Do you want to host the glory? Let Him elevate you to the level of "whatever."

"Therefore I tell you, <u>whatever</u> you ask for in prayer, believe that you have received it, and it will be yours." (Mark 11:24)

Another word I received from the Lord as I cried out for His Glory was, "If you want more face time with the Lord, spend more time face down on the floor." Now, I know that some people physically can't do this? It is not some new legalistic thing. The Lord will make a way.

Ask, knock, and seek! The Lord isn't looking for us to do something glorious. He is doing the glorious things right now and He isn't sharing His glory with any man or woman. There are so many wonderful Psalms of praise that open the way for the Glory to come.

"Shout for joy to the Lord, all the earth. Worship the Lord with gladness; come before him with joyful songs. Know that the Lord is God. It is he who made us, and we are his; we are his people, the sheep of his pasture. Enter his gates with thanksgiving and his courts with praise; give thanks to him and praise his name. For the Lord is good and his love endures forever; his faithfulness continues through all generations." (Psalm 100)

I want to conclude with one final note from the Word of God. Read it aloud, meditate on it, and choose where you will stand! Amen and Amen!

"Nevertheless the solid foundation of God stands, having this seal: 'The Lord knows those who are His,' and, 'Let everyone who names the name of Christ depart from

iniquity.' But in a great house there are not only vessels of gold and silver, but also of wood and clay, some for honor and some for dishonor. Therefore if anyone cleanses himself from the latter, he will be a vessel for honor, sanctified and useful for the Master, prepared for every good work." (2 Timothy 2:19-21)

OTHER BOOKS BY THIS AUTHOR:

"A Warrior's Guide to the Seven Spirits of God" - Part 1: Basic Training, by James A. Durham, Copyright © James A. Durham, printed by Xulon Press, August 2011.

"A Warrior's Guide to the Seven Spirits of God" - Part 2: Advanced Individual Training, by James A. Durham, Copyright © James A. Durham, printed by Xulon Press, August 2011.

"Beyond the Ancient Door" – Free to Move About the Heavens, by James A. Durham, Copyright © James A. Durham, printed by Xulon Press, August 2012.

CPSIA information can be obtained at www.ICGtesting.com
Printed in the USA
BVOW070138300812

299111BV00001B/4/P